MAN,

KNOW THYSELF

AGAIN

Philosophical and Educational Concepts From

Ancient Kemet

Kofi Khepera

Table of Contents

PART I: THE AFRIKAN WRITERS

iii

PART II: THE NON-AFRIKAN WRITERS

PART III: THE PEOPLE OF KEMET

Dedication

To the Ancestors, Elders, Sistahs, and Brothas of the Great Afrikan Family. I hope that you are pleased with what your New Born Sun has put on these pages in the struggle for the betterment of Our Nation, Our Family. I love you all. Ankh, udja, seneb (life, prosperity, and health)...

Acknowledgments

Hotep. I need to first give thanks and praise to and acknowledge the presence of the Creator and Ancestors. Without them, I would not and could not exist. To Ancestor Nana Baffour Amankwatia II (Dr. Asa G. Hilliard III), thank you for the inspiration to become an educational psychologist. I am extremely thankful for all of the tremendous work you have done on education in Kmt and for all Afrikans.

To Ancestor Dr. Amos N. Wilson, thank you for making it plain; for presenting your magnificent work in a way that all Afrikans can absorb, understand, and act on. To Ancestor Dr. John Henrik Clarke, I cannot thank you enough for your shining example of Afrikan eldership and relentless pursuit of truth for the Afrikan world.

To Ancestor Dr. John G. Jackson, I am indebted to you for the clarity and truth you gave our people about religion and its Afrikan origin. To Ancestor Dr. Yosef A. A. ben-Jochannan, thank you for being you and being so unapologetically Afrikan. Thank you for bringing the truth about our Family to light with such love and passion. To Ancestor Dr. Cheikh Anta Diop, your work has meant more to the Afrikan world than words can ever express. Our people will forever thank and honor you for working relentlessly to restore our past to its proper place.

To Baba Dr. Runoko Rashidi, I am and will be forever grateful to you for pushing and challenging me to go further. Without you nudging me, I do not know that this book would have materialized. To Dr. Marimba Ani, your work on Afrikan spirituality and consciousness helped to light my path so I could find my way back to my Afrikanity. To Dr. Rkhty Amen, your work on Kmt: the language, people, way of life, and assistance with Kemetic terms was instrumental in my creating this book.

I have to give a special thank you to my jegna, Sister Carnita (Dr. Carnita Groves). Your unwavering support, honesty, and dedication to my well-being as an Afrikan man is appreciated more than you know. I hope that I can repay you for your love and guidance. Thank you all for the instrumental roles you have played and continue to play in the development of the Afrikan consciousness, and for the legacy of wisdom, knowledge, love, and guidance you provide for the beloved Afrikan Family. Asante sana...

Preface

"Education has but one honorable purpose, one alone, everything else is a waste of time. The role of education is to train the student to be a responsible handler of power."

- Ancestor Dr. John Henrik Clarke

"Education is crucial in any type of society for the preservation of the lives of its members and the maintenance of the social structure."

- Ancestor Dr. Walter Rodney – How Europe Underdeveloped Africa

This book is meant to be a compilation comprised of the main points taken from the texts of both Afrikan and non-Afrikan writers split into three parts. Parts one and two specifically deal with the various aspects of educational and philosophical concepts that were developed in ancient Kmt/Kemet (Egypt). Those works found in part one were written by Afrikan scholars and master teachers, while part two contains those works composed by non-Afrikan writers. As I read through the works of both Afrikan and non-Afrikan authors, I began identifying and selecting information from each author with those Afrikans who may be new to or just beginning their journey through Afrikan history and culture in mind.

Part three of this work briefly details our Kemetic ancestors in so far as what they looked like (*phenotype*) and how they lived as a society. It is by no means an exhaustive review of either subject. I felt that it was necessary to incorporate information from both present day writers, and those in antiquity who witnessed the Kemetic people's phenotype and how they lived. Afrikans around the world today just as in the past, are constantly being inundated with Eurocentric thought and opinion concerning whether or not our Kemetic

Ancestors were Black Afrikans and the role of the Afrikan woman and education in Kemetic society, so the importance of part three seemed obvious to me.

Our Afrikan Ancestors, all of those thousands of years ago, explained the importance of having a knowledge of one's self and of learning. We of the Afrikan collective today cannot afford to feel any differently. The Ancestors take immense pride in their roles as educators to this very day. This pride was not and is not due to an inflated ego or feelings of superiority. The way that our Ancestors developed and disseminated, and applied knowledge was second to none in the ancient world.

It is my hope that, like myself, the Afrikan family will find the passion; the desire; the will to nurture, preserve, and protect our land, knowledge, culture, and ways of life; to reconnect, rediscover, and to build upon the work that our Ancestors started thousands of years ago. The never-ending hunger to know more about and to fully embrace my Afrikanity through learning about the Ancestors; learning about their accomplishments, their failures, triumphs, and tragedies, resulted in gorging myself on a buffet of books about Afrika written by Master Teachers.

From those pivotal works I was able to attempt a work of my own. It is in these pages that I hope, in some way, more of the great Afrikan Family is encouraged and inspired to begin or continue their journey of self-knowledge and ultimately... love of and respect for ourselves and our people.

Kofi Khepera

2020

PART I:

THE

AFRIKAN

WRITERS

DR. NTERI RENENET ELSON

BRIEF AUTHOR BIO

- Reiki master & Holistic Psychotherapist

- 25+ years of private practice experience

- Author & Lecturer

- 30+ years in fields of behavioral & mental health

- Fmr. Adj. Prof. - Afrikana Studies - UMass.

- Mdu Ntr (medu neter) symbologist

- Co-founder & Instructor - Academy of Kemetic Education Right Relationship Right Knowledge, Maat Inc.

Source: rightrelationshiprightknowledge.net/bios.html

MERKABA:

THE GREAT PYRAMID

IS THE TREE OF LIFE

MANUSCRIPT TYPE: Book

Main points from the text:

a. The Kemites developed a knowledge of a science of the soul and were master psychologists/spiritual practitioners.

b. Kemetic scholars had developed the three mdu nTr; Ka Ab Ba, for (Elson, 2015):

- An understanding of the spiritual and physical anatomy of Man, Woman, Cosmos.

- Unlocking the psychological and spiritual journey while unfolding our consciousness.

- Liberating the soul from that which would impede it on its path.

c. The Kemites developed symbols to represent sacred concepts, such as Khepera (representing the creation of the Universe) (Elson, 2015).

DR. WADE NOBLES

BRIEF AUTHOR BIO

- Fmr. President & Co-founder - Association of Black Psychologists (ABPsi).

- Over 100 publications credited to him.

- Studied under Ancestor Baba Credo Mutwa in South Africa

- 40+ years studying ancient Afrikan philosophy

- Prof. Emer. - Africana Studies & Black Psychology - SFSU.

- Conducted 80+ nationally funded development research projects

Source: drwadenobles.com/bio

PER AA ASA HILLIARD: THE GREAT HOUSE OF BLACK LIGHT FOR EDUCATIONAL EXCELLENCE

MANUSCRIPT TYPE: Research article

Main Points from the Text:

a. The oft quoted "Man, know thyself" was not first uttered or thought of by Socrates at all. Rather, that phrase was an important admonition amongst the scholars and teachers of Kmt (Nobles, 2008).

b. The native African Kemetic dynasties 1-12, 18, and 25 were ruled by per-Aas with an insatiable thirst for knowledge.

c. During Dynasty 18 in Waset, Ipet Isut (Karnak) was the epicenter of Kemetic education.

- Ipet Isut means *the most select or holiest of places* (Hilliard III, 1995).

- The meaning of the name Ipet Isut spoke to the high level of importance that the ancient Kemites placed on education.

d. Ipet Isut had a student population upwards of over 80,000 students (Nobles, 2008).

e. The name given to the staff or teachers at Ipet Isut was Hersetha, meaning "teachers of the mysteries" (Hilliard III, 1995, p.730).

f. The Hersetha were split according to what they taught.

- Those who taught astronomy or astrology were mystery teachers of heaven, and those who taught philosophy and theology were mystery teachers of the secret word.

g. The ancient Kemites had no concept of inferior intellectual capacity. Their surroundings were constructed such that they became living classrooms, with the teachers leading their students by example; demonstrating what needed to be learned.

h. Grammar, rhetoric (persuasive speaking), logic, arithmetic (type of mathematics), music, and astronomy were the "Kemetic Liberal Arts" (Hilliard III, 1995).

i. Education in Kmt was not merely learning for learning's sake.

   - The process of education in Kmt was meant to assist individuals in journeying toward becoming more 'god like' (Nobles, 2008).

j. Education and learning were believed by the Kemites to be methods of igniting or awakening the divinity within humanity.

DR. RKHTY AMEN

BRIEF AUTHOR BIO

- Kemetologist & linguist

- 30+ years teaching mdu nTr (medu neter)

- Authored several publications & 5 books

- Dir. of Kemetic Philology

- Lectured on multiple continents

- Co-founder of The Kemetic Institute in Chicago

- Teaches mdu nTr at University of Kemetian Sciences

Source: meduneter.com/instructors

A LIFE CENTERED LIFE
LIVING MAAT

MANUSCRIPT TYPE: Book

Main Points from the Text:

a. Maat is the first known form of education all Kemites received and was the foundation of all other education given (Amen, 2012).

 ▪ Kemetic parents gave the education of Maat with their children even before they were born.

 ▪ Like many parents today, the Kemites too spoke to their children while still in the womb.

b. Both men and women were taught to read and write from a young age (Amen, 2012).

c. The education of Maat was taught to the children by the mothers first, then to the extended family.

- Maat was not just taught as a theoretical concept; it was applied and repeatedly demonstrated in the home and throughout Kemetic society, thus showing how to live life in Kmt.

d. Maat was required learning prior to receiving any other education.

e. The principles of Maat were: Right, Truth, Justice, Good, Balance, Compassion (Amen, 2012).

f. Maat was taught to all students in order to study and understand the relationship between all things.

g. Kmt was unquestionably a *literate* society.

DR. ITIBARI M. ZULU

BRIEF AUTHOR BIO

- Africologist & Librarian

- Wrote & published numerous articles

- Th.D. - African world religions - Amen-Ra Theological Seminary – L.A.

- Exec.Ed. - Journal of Pan African Studies

- MLIS - Library and Information Science – SJSU

THE ANCIENT KEMETIC ROOTS OF LIBRARY & INFORMATION SCIENCE

MANUSCRIPT TYPE: Research article

Main Points from the Text:

a. The Kemites were the earliest known people to build the world's first known major libraries and higher learning establishments.

b. Kemetic scholars had created the earliest known library classification system several thousand years before the Dewey Decimal System came into being (Zulu, 2012).

c. Ancient Kemetic temples contained what is thought to be the first organized library collections (Amen, 1975; Zulu, 2012).

d. Library collections were public as well as private; being kept in schools, palaces, temples, and so on.

e. Two Kemetic librarians, a father and son, whose tombs were found in Waset (Thebes to the Greeks); Neb-Nufre and Nufre-Heteb, provide proof of the profession of librarian-priest (Zulu, 2012).

   ▪ Neb-Nufre and Nufre-Heteb's tombs provide striking evidence that librarianship was passed down; inherited through one's family.

f. These librarian-priests attended professional library and religious education institutions (Zulu, 2012).

g. Ramses II was the chief library builder in Kmt, and can be referred to as the dean of library sciences.

h. Rameses II is credited with constructing the:

- Hypostyle Hall at Karnak, rock temple-library of Abu-Simbel, temple-library of Aabdju (Abydos), temple-library at Waset (Luxor), the Ramesseum funerary temple-library at Waset (Zulu, 2012, p. 8).

i. The library at Edfu was referred to as the *House of Papyrus*; the *House of Tablet*; the *House of Sacred Writing* (Zulu, 2012).

j. The Kemites often combined the functions of libraries, universities, and temples into a singular body; a temple-library-university.

k. Nana Baffour Amankwatia II (Dr. Asa G. Hilliard III) proclaimed that Ipet Isut contained the most highly developed education system ever recorded during the ancient epoch.

- Dr. Van Sertima (1985) also confirmed the total student population at Ipet Isut was approximately 80,000 from all grade levels.

l. Several other scholars, such as Thompson (1940), Dunlap (1991), Metzger (1980), and Richardson (1914) all asserted Kmt to be the birthplace of libraries.

m. Titles often given to Kemetic librarians were (Zulu, 2012):

- Custodians of the unlimited knowledge

- Seshu (scribes) of the house of sacred writings (Shedmeszer and Messuri)

- Seshu of the house of the archives of Per-Aa (Neferhor)

- Seshu of the gods

- Seshu of the sacred book

- Seshu of the mdu nTr (hieroglyphs)

- Keeper of the scrolls

DR. JOHN G. JACKSON

BRIEF AUTHOR BIO

- Co-authored *A Guide to the Study of African History* with Dr. Willis N. Huggins

- Published 10+ books and pamphlets

- Wrote for Marcus Garvey's Newspaper, *Negro World* as a high school student

- Fmr. Assoc. Dir. – [Edward Wilmot] Blyden Society

- Was a student of master teachers Hubert Henry Harrison, Arthur Schomburg, J.A. Rogers, and Dr. Willis N. Huggins

---

Sources:
aalbc.com/authors/
Runoko Rashidi's African Star Over Asia: The Black Presence in the East

INTRODUCTION TO AFRICAN CIVILIZATIONS

MANUSCRIPT TYPE: Book

Main Points from the Text:

a. The Library at Alexandria had three specific goals, which were (Jackson, 2001):

  • (1) Maintenance and conservation of knowledge still in existence. (2) Increase of said knowledge. (3) Circulation of said knowledge.

b. The Museum at Alexandria was a university, comprised of teachers of astronomy, mathematics, literature, and medicine (Jackson, 2001).

c. The genesis or beginning of "formal" education was in the form of spoken tradition in Afrika, and was delivered during initiation rituals.

d. A knowledge of music existed in "prehistoric" Afrika (Jackson, 2001).

e. Early Afrikans engaged in the precise research of both animals and plants.

f. Research of animals resulted in progress toward animal husbandry (breed/care for farm animals).

g. From researching plants, the path to agriculture was opened up.

h. The Edfu text found at the temple of Edfu relays the account of civilization being brought into Kmt from the south by a group of blacksmiths who were the followers of King Heru (Horus to the Greeks) (Jackson, 2001).

i. There are ruins in Somaliland that were built with dressed stone and bear a resemblance to early Kemetic architecture.

j. The education of the blacksmiths of Somaliland would have passed into Kmt some time before 5,000 B.C.E.

k. The Ancestors of the Kemites possessed weapons and tools at that time in antiquity.

l. Herodotus stated that Kemetic women were knowledgeable of and engaged in trade at the marketplaces, while their husbands would remain at home (Jackson, 2001).

m. Pre-dynastic Kemites were already engaging in trade with other nations.

THE GOLDEN AGES OF AFRICA

MANUSCRIPT TYPE: Book

Main Points from the Text:

a. The arts and sciences came down the Hapi (Nile) from Kush and Nubia into Kmt.

b. Regarding the development of Hor-em-akhet, the Great Pyramid, and Kemetic scientific knowledge, Egyptologist Gerald Massey observed :

> *"A study of the Sphinx and the Great Pyramid by several modern scholars has revealed to us the great scientific knowledge possessed by the Egyptians six thousand years ago"* (Jackson, 1987, p. 31).

c. On the topics of both Kemetic earth measurements and French astronomer and geodesist, Gian Domenico Cassini, Peter Tompkins (1971) commented that:

> *"Cassini, who...proposed the adoption of the geodetic foot representing 1/6000th part of a terrestrial minute of arc, would have been astounded had he known that such a foot had been in existence for several millennia* [in Kmt]"

Tompkins continued:

> *"...the Sphinx... also once had an obelisk between its paws, whose shadow could be used to compute not only the correct circumference of the earth, but the variance in the degree of latitude"* (Cassini, 1971, p. 33).

d. The representations of the zodiacal and other constellations are ideograms that bear strong similarities to the ideograms in the mdu nTr (Jackson, 1987).

e. The Ancestors of the Kemites possessed weapons and tools at that time in antiquity.

- See Dr. John G. Jackson's citation of Nino del Grande's *Prehistoric Iron Smelting in Africa.*

AGES OF

GOLD AND SILVER

MANUSCRIPT TYPE: Book

Main Points from the Text:

a. First century C.E. Greek philosopher Apollonius of Tyana was educated in by Kemetic priests.

- According to Greek philosopher Theophrastrus, Apollonius stated that Pythagoras was educated by the Kemites, who were before educated by the Kushites (Jackson, 1990).

b. The Kemites had already made substantial progress in the fields of astronomy and geometry before the arrival of Menes.

c. The solar year was first developed and divided into twelve periods in Kmt.

- Greek historian and traveler Herodotus stated that the Kemites were the first to develop the leap year.

d. The Kemites developed the knowledge of the sun as the center of the universe (Jackson, 1990).

- They also figured out that earth and the other planets revolved around the sun in permanent orbital positions.

- In addition, the Kemites were well aware of the fact that the moon revolved around the earth.

e. The power of gravitation was known and taught in Kmt.

- Pythagoras was given this knowledge by the Kemetic priest Oenuphis of On (Heliopolis to the Greeks) (Jackson, 1990).

f. Orientalist Robert Brown stated that the Kemites had developed use of the telescope.

DR. GEORGE G.M. JAMES

BRIEF AUTHOR BIO

- Asserted that Greek philosophy is copied/stolen ancient Egyptian philosophy

- Died mysteriously after writing and publishing *Stolen Legacy*

- Was Prof. of Logic and Greek – Livingstone College – NC

- Received Ph.D. from Columbia University – NY

- *Stolen Legacy* ignited several debates about Afrikan influence on the Greeks.

STOLEN LEGACY: GREEK PHILOSOPHY IS STOLEN EGYPTIAN PHILOSOPHY

MANUSCRIPT TYPE: Book

Main Points from the Text:

a. The Kemetic Mystery (education) System was the cultural epicenter (headquarters) of Kmt; similar to how the University serves that purpose today.

   ▪ There were three "grades" of students who entered into the Kemetic Mystery System (James, 2001):

      • *The Mortals* (trial students in a sense).

- *The Intelligences* (those who have achieved an inner vision).

- *The Creators* or *Sons of Light* (those identified with true spiritual consciousness).

  - For a number of years, the students had to endure various scholarly tests.

b. After around 5,000 years of refusing to allow Greeks entry or to give them any sort of Kemetic education in large numbers, Greeks were finally allowed access to Kemetic education (James, 2001).

  - This happened through a series of two invasions; the Persians (ca.525 B.C.E.) and the Greeks themselves (ca. 332 B.C.E.), wherein the immigration laws in Kmt were drastically changed.

c. The doctrines that Pythagoras receives credit for developing originated in Kmt, specifically, the Kemetic Mystery System of learning (James, 2001).

- Like all others before him, Pythagoras had to gain the approval of the priests in Kmt to be initiated.

- Pythagoras was taught concepts, such as geometry (including properties of the right angled triangle), medicine, dietetics (study of the diet), music, and metempsychosis (James, 2001).

  - The idea of metempsychosis is the migration of one's soul at death to a new body or vessel. This was nowhere to be found in Greek religion until after Pythagoras learned it in Kmt and brought it back to Greece.

d. Plato, in his work *Timaeus*, reported that those Greeks yearning to acquire wisdom visited Kmt for initiation, where the priests of Sau (Sais to the Greeks) thought of and called them amateurs or absolute beginners in the Mysteries (education system) (James, 2001).

- Philosopher and politician Hermodorus of Syracuse (ca. fourth century B.C.E.) also wrote that Plato visited Kmt for the specific purpose of receiving an education.

- Plato's doctrine of the *Nous* or the World Soul is a Kemetic truth of magic.

- The genesis of Plato's doctrine of Demiurge (a creator of the world) and the story of creation that originated in Kmt ca. 4000 B.C.E.

e. The priests of Kmt admitted individuals into the education system in order to encourage spiritual growth.

f. Thales was among those Greeks who were initiated into Kmt's education system (James, 2001).

- Thales was taught astronomy, land surveying, mensuration (measurement), engineering, and Kemetic theology.

g. Greek philosopher Democritus of Miletus (ca. 400 B.C.E.) also traveled to Kmt for the purpose of receiving an education from the priests.

- Herodotus and Diogenes both reported that Democritus stayed five years in Kmt learning the priests. Once his studies were finished, Democritus wrote a book about the writing script of Meroe.

h. All of Socrates' doctrines link him to the Kemetic Mysteries system of education in Kmt (James, 2001).

- The phrase "Man know thyself," often attributed to Socrates, was taken from inscriptions found outside of Kemetic temples of learning.

- Socrates' doctrine of *Nous* (the Mind) originated in Kmt, where Asr (Osiris) was represented on the temples by an open eye; the *All Seeing Eye*. The eye was representative of sight that goes far beyond time and space but also the omniscience of the Creator.

- Socrates' idea of the *Supreme Good* also originated in Kmt. There, the idea of the *Supreme Good* that Socrates spoke of is the earliest concept of salvation.

i. Aristotle's doctrines too, find their origins in Kmt.

- His doctrine of *Being*, for example, has its beginnings in Kemetic scholarship, as the Kemites were believed to be the first known people to discover the principle of duality in nature.

- The doctrine of the attributes of nature stated that nature is comprised of motion and rest, moving from imperfection to perfection.

  - The Kemetic creation story showed exactly that, with nature moving from chaos gradually into a state of order.

- Aristotle's *doctrine of the soul* asserted that the soul is a "radical principle of life", possessing five attributes (James, 2001, p. 117).

  - The source of Aristotle's doctrine of the soul too has been traced back to the Kemetic *Book of Coming Forth by Day and by Night* (Book of the Dead).

j. Under Emperor Theodosius in the fourth century C.E. and Emperor Justinian in the sixth century C.E., many of the temple-universities and schools in Kmt were closed down permanently.

k. Per-Aa Wahibre Psamtik (Psammitichus to the Greeks) is thought to have been responsible for the appearance of the Demotic form of writing, and for it being used for commercial and trade reasons (James, 2001).

l. *Senzar* was one of the names given to ways of speaking by the priests who were a part of the mysteries education system in Kmt.

m. The Kemites assigned number values and words to geometrical figures; modeling the intention, it appeared, of how they used mdu nTr (hieroglyphs) (James, 2001).

n. The curriculum of the mysteries system in Kmt in part consisted of the seven liberal arts (James, 2001).

- Grammar, rhetoric, and logic were taught to get rid of a person's senseless or illogical behaviors.

- Geometry and arithmetic assisted, in part, in understanding the problems of a person's nature and existence.

- Astronomy was taught to handle the invisible mental energies within people and nations.

- Music (Harmony) was taught to help the student to regulate their life so that it is in harmony with the Creator. Music in Kmt had a healing quality to it as it evidenced by the fact that Kemetic priests utilized it to cure diseases.

o. New students who entered the Kemetic education system were required to exhibit specific attributes.

p. Salvation of one's soul was thought to have been the purpose of philosophy in Kmt.

- This salvation, of course, was accomplished in part through purification offered in the Kemetic Mystery System.

- Going through this process took an individual from mortal to the immortal stage.

q. Kemetic scholars taught that the human body was a prison for the soul; the soul being trapped there.

- Kemetic scholars maintained that the trapping of the soul caused the cycle of rebirth/reincarnation.

r. In order to study in Kmt, one had to undergo circumcision, which many of the Greek learners did.

- Origen, a native of Kmt, wrote *"No one among the Egyptians, either studied geometry, or investigated the secrets of astronomy, unless circumcision had been undertaken"* (James, 2001, p. 44).

s. Secret libraries filled with manuscripts could have been found within each of the temples throughout Kmt.

- The Persians, Greeks, and Romans all raided the secret libraries during their respective invasions.

t. So-called Greek philosophical thought was a completely foreign concept to the Greeks and their then social and political conditions. Several Greek philosophers were being indicted by the Athenian government for introducing foreign philosophical ideas. Socretes, Anaxagoras, Diagoras, Aspasia, and Euripides all were indicted for their *"new beliefs"* that went against the Greek state.

- This provides an accurate description of the social environment amongst the Greeks from 640 – 332 B.C.E., which is from the time of Thales to Aristotle. The Greeks were plagued by civil wars, constant threats of and actual invasion by the Persians, and their own government's hostile position toward new philosophical thought and ideas. Therefore, the conditions made it highly unlikely that Greece would have given birth to any philosophers or produced their own philosophy during this time.

DR. ASA G. HILLIARD III

BRIEF AUTHOR BIO

- Also known as Nana Baffour Amankwatia II

- Afrikan historian & author of over 1,000 publications including 8 books.

- Fmr. superintendent of schools in Monrovia, Liberia

- Received Ph.D. from University of Denver

- Was a board certified forensic examiner – Testified in cases regarding test validity and biasness

Sources: sites.gsu.edu/asahilliard/about/

THE MAROON WITHIN US

MANUSCRIPT TYPE: Book

Main Points from the Text:

a. While Africans were being enslaved in the American North and South, there were those Africans who escaped and formed "maroon" nations.

- Several maroon nations were never conquered and showed an immense amount of pride in their cultural ancestry. The concept of the *maroon* or *maroonage* was freedom with the intent of maintaining cultural continuity (Hilliard III, 1995).

b. Many of the very important aspects of Kemetic education were conducted in secret.

c. A great deal of the tradition involved in the heavily guarded knowledge was passed on orally.

d. There was an almost perfect balance between education and the spiritual beliefs of the Kemites. This balance was extended to politics, economics, and so on (Hilliard III, 1995).

e. Due to their natural environment, the Kemites were in an extremely advantageous position to make countless observations of nature over many thousands of years.

- Through careful observation, the Kemites were able to (within reason) predict the behavior (rise and fall) of the Hapi (Nile) River.

f. Due to often having clear skies, the Kemites were able to once again carry out painstaking observations; this time, it was of the stars and their placement and movement.

g. The Kemites' view of technology was that it should only be utilized to better understand mankind's relationship to and place in nature (Hilliard III, 1995).

h. The ultimate objective of education in Kmt was to become one with the Creator, or to become like the Creator.

i. Students of the Kemetic Mysteries System were seeking the 10 virtues, which are:

- (1) Control of thought. (2) Control of actions. (3) Steadfastness of purpose. (4) Identity with the spiritual life. (5) Evidence of having a mission in life. (6) Evidence of a call to spiritual orders. (7) Freedom from resentment under persecution and wrong. (8) Confidence in the power of the master as teacher. (9) Confidence in one's own ability to learn. (10) Readiness or preparedness for initiation (Hilliard III, 1995, p. 92-93).

These virtues were/are not a part of the Western European educational structure that many of us have been subjected to.

j. Waset (Thebes to the Greeks/Luxor to the Arabs) was considered the base or headquarters of *higher* education in all of Kmt.

- There also is mention of another "grand lodge," named the Osirica that was located in Lower (Northern) Kmt, which was dedicated to the manifestation of the Creator, Asr (Hilliard III, 1995).

k. The Osirica had a powerful effect on a number of Greek lodges that appeared later.

l. During the occupation of Kmt by the Hyksos, art and architecture had suffered.

- The education of Kemites, on the other hand, carried on as it had before the invasion by the Hyksos.

m. Job training was not the main focus of education in Kmt. This was only a small part.

n. The higher goals of the Kemetic and ancient African educational system were (Hilliard III, 1995):

- (1) Unity of person, unity of the tribe, and unity of all with nature. (2) Development of social responsibility. (3) Development of character. (4) Development of spiritual power.

- Highest goal was to become godlike through the revision of one's own nTr of how the Creator is revealed in the person

- The Kemites appeared have given very little consideration to what the concept of a person being intellectually incompetent.

- A considerable amount of thought was given to character; its development, interference, or promotion of a person's educational development.

o. Education in Kmt allowed for people's resurrection as a new person by putting them through consecutive personal and social changes.

p. A great deal of time and focus was spent on stories, investigation of symbols and signs, use of proverbs, and use of songs and dance in Kemetic schools (Hilliard III, 1995).

q. The fundamental belief in all things being interconnected allowed for such analogies to be used as powerful tools in Kemetic education.

r. A student's living environment was utilized and organized to be used in teaching.

s. The education process was a religious one, in the sense that it was deeply immersed in Kemetic spiritual thought.

t. The "lower" education system, meaning education outside of the Mysteries, whether strictly organized or not, allowed for organic development.

- Students studying advanced education could decide between higher tier leadership positions in society or to take the path of a scholar and pursue knowledge and wisdom.

u. *Serious* education of Kemetic students included putting them in situations to be a direct observer of nature. The students were often paired with teachers or masters as apprentices (Hilliard III, 1995).

v. The reasoning for Kemetic apprenticeship was to learn and understand the laws of matter.

   ▪ This knowledge separated master craftsman from general workers.

w. The overall notion pushed by European scholars that Kemetic seshu (scribes) were arrogant and thought of themselves superior is false.

   ▪ See the writing of Ptahhotep (1987) – Fifth Dynasty (ca. 2350 B.C.E.)

x. The focus of all education in Kmt was nature, and the people's connection to it.

- Nature in turn played a large role in the spiritual beliefs of the Kemites.

y. Due to Kmt's advanced society, it required that they have highly educated individuals; even those who were not in advanced studies were very well educated.

z. Every temple in Kmt had a faculty and a librarian on site. Librarians were an important part of society during the Old Kingdom period (ca: 2665 – 2160 B.C.E.) (Hilliard III, 1995).

aa. Librarians in Kmt were found as far back as the Fourth Dynasty (ca. 2613 B.C.E.)

bb. Education in Kmt was "open enrollment". Education was not at all linked to ancestry, as many European scholars maintain.

- The example of Amenhotep is given. He was of *lowly* birth, and yet he designed the plans for Ipet Isut (Hilliard III, 1995).

- The per-Aa's children, like the rest of the children in Kmt, had to adhere to a difficult path of intense study on their own.

THE TEACHINGS OF PTAHHOTEP: THE OLDEST BOOK IN THE WORLD

MANUSCRIPT TYPE: Book

Main Points from the Text:

a. Mdu nTr appears fully developed without any trace of a formative stage of development.

- It appears to have been in existence for a considerable amount of time prior to Ta-Seti or Kmt forming as nations.

b. The earliest writings developed in Kmt were regarding lists of offerings to the Deity or the manifestations of it (Ptahhotep, Hilliard III, Williams, & Damali, 1987).

c. The recording of declaration of virtues came about during the Old Kingdom period (ca. 2665 – 2160 B.C.E.).

- From this practice came the 42 Negative Confessions, during the eighteenth dynasty of the New Kingdom period (ca. 1554 – 1190 B.C.E.) (Ptahhotep et al., 1987).

- These declarations can be found inside the *Per-em-Heru* (*The Book of Coming Forth From Darkness Into Light*).

- The Commandments found in the Old Testament look quite similar to the 42 Negative Confessions.

d. The oldest and complete Wisdom text is the Teachings of Ptahhotep (Ptahhotep et al., 1987).

- Ptahhotep's teachings were written 2,500 years before the time of Jesus the Christ.

- Ptahhotep was reported to have been 110 years of age when he wrote this text.

e. Consistent with descriptions of Kemetic education where a choice is given in higher education between a political life and a priestly one; Ptahhotep chose the latter.

f. Rather than claiming to be the author of these teachings, Ptahhotep attributed the wisdom in this text to his people, and to the Creator or Deity (Ptahhotep et al., 1987).

- It was believed that the teachings were written by manifestations of the Creator.

- Ancestor Hilliard asked the following salient questions (Ptahhotep et al., 1987, p. 38):

  - *What was barbaric or heathenistic about Ptahhotep?*

  - *Why were his and other Kemetic scholars' writing ordered destroyed?.*

SBA:

REAWAKENING OF

THE AFRICAN MIND

MANUSCRIPT TYPE: Book

Main Points from the Text:

a. The Kemetic term *sbA* in the Kemetic language means study and teachings (Hilliard III, 1998).

- *sbA* is seen first during the Old Kingdom/Pyramid Age, and again later during the Middle Kingdom.

- *siA* in the Kemetic language means insight; *sbA* leads to *siA*.

- *wHmy msw* means the reawakening in the Kemetic language. Without combining *mDu nTr* and *mDu nfr*, *wHmy msw* cannot happen.

b. Once *mDu nfr* is mastered by the student, will lead to the use of *mDu nTr* meaning divine speech.

c. When one studies the text, *The Teachings of Ptahhotep,* they will discover that 14 of the 37 teachings taught and discussed matters of non-violence (Hilliard III, 1998).

d. In Kmt, identification with the divine was of the utmost importance. The struggle to identify with the Creator was expressed in Kmt as *maAt*.

- To the Kemites, *maAt* is concerned with all 5 spheres of reality (Hilliard III, 1998, p. 12):

  • Divine or Sacred world, Cosmos or Universe, State or the Governance, Society or Human Community (Humanity), Human Beings (Family).

- Each reality had 5 dimensions of significance (Hilliard III, 1998, p. 12):

- Religious, Cosmic, Political, Social, Anthropological.

e. In Kmt, the law of *maAt* stated that all of the sciences are connected to one another (Hilliard III, 1998; Obenga, 1996).

- Possessing a philosophy and system of divine spirituality with everything being interrelated in some way, the Kemetic people developed a civilization and way of life linked to the sacred and divine.

f. The Kemites were continually striving to be in tune with nature and the divine. As a result, seshu (scribes), such as Ptahhotep, would have asked the Creator for permission to perform divinely sanctioned and spiritual tasks, like teaching.

g. There were at least six known aims of teaching in Kmt (Hilliard III, 1998).

- The first aim was to do away with conflict among the people; to develop harmony and order.

- A second aim of teaching in Kmt was to ensure that both the east and west banks of the Hapi served the Creator were in the likeness of Ra, and could be linked to the Creator both in behavior and purpose.

- The development of wisdom was a third aim of teaching in Kmt.

  - There was a divine charge in Kmt that stated "no one is born wise" (Hilliard III, 1998, p. 81)

- Teaching a knowledge and conceptual understanding of the standards of *mDu nfr* (good or beautiful speech) was vitally important to the development of one's character.

- Concerning future generations, learning that which will benefit and educating those who follow you, established an obligation of teachers across generations; a fourth aim of teaching in Kmt.

- Being able to *hear* the extraordinary message of what is being taught was a fifth aim of education.

- Expressing virtuous behavior(s) in line with *maAt* is the sixth aim of education.

h. The people of Kmt were extremely dependent upon writing (Hilliard III, 1998).

- Evidence of this can be seen in the writings on the walls, sarcophagi, papyri, monuments, and jewelry throughout Kmt and its history.

i. Two aspects of the scribal education and socialization process in Kmt are (Hilliard III, 1998):

- The scribal education process was reliant upon "great works" for material. Seshu spent countless hours copying them.

- The basic method of scribal education was an apprenticeship.

j. For a period of almost 650 years of Greek and Roman occupation, the Kemetic culture and society kept a tight grip on the minds of their invaders.

- The foundations of Europe's classical civilization came from the modified religious and educational systems of the Kemites.

D. N. SIFUNA
&
J. E. OTIENDE

BRIEF AUTHOR BIO

- Daniel Sifuna is Prof. of Educational Foundations – Kenyatta University

- James Otiende is Senior Lecturer – Kenyatta University

Sources:

africanbookscollective.com/books/an-introductory-history-of-education

biography.omicsonline.org/kenya/kenyatta-university/prof-daniel-namusonge-sifuna-873472

AN INTRODUCTORY HISTORY OF EDUCATION

MANUSCRIPT TYPE: Book

Main Points from the Text:

a. Religion was an integral part of art, science, and technology in Kmt. Everything was connected to religion in some way.

b. The educational aims in Kmt were about preservation of a stable society and the then social conditions (Sifuna & Otiende, 2006).

   ■ The social structure was split into three distinct classes: Upper (the Royal family, nobles, and priests), Middle (scribes and other professionals), and Lower (fellahins and slaves).

- The priest oversaw the entirety of Kmt's education system.

- Education strengthened the socially stratified aspect of Kmt's society.

c. The Kemites developed both religious and philosophical concepts to enhance and solidify their influence on Kemetic education.

d. Regarding the purpose of education in Kmt, Sifuna and Otiende noted:

   "It was practical, technical, and professional and sought to produce professionals and work-oriented personnel for propping the social, economic, political and religious structures of Egypt..." (Sifuna & Otiende, 2006, p. 20).

e. The development of Kmt's education system led to an intricate agricultural science, and the advancement of irrigation and flood control systems.

- Tools, such as the nilometer, were used in irrigation and flood control.

- Agricultural engineers had to figure out the size and strength of the various components of an irrigation or flood system (dykes, bridges, etc.) that they constructed.

f. Education was also defined as practical and designed to be useful in Kmt. Through their education system, the Kemites were able to realize their religious beliefs of polytheism (Sifuna & Otiende, 2006).

g. Kemetic education was a means for the Kemites to enhance their religious and moral development.

h. Elementary education developed in Kmt as a result of fundamental societal needs.

- By 1000 B.C.E., the Kemites tailored formal education to match the various socially stratified classes of the Kemetic population (Sifuna & Otiende, 2006).

i. The economic and political demands in Kmt created a need for professionally trained clerks, copyists, computers, and inspectors.

j. Due to having an agriculturally driven economy, there was need for producing agricultural mechanics (Sifuna & Otiende, 2006).

k. With the advent of a writing system, the seshu (scribes) in Kmt began recording their accomplishments in the fields of science, art, etc.

- Boys who were given the opportunity to go to school learned about the scientific and artistic accomplishments of their people.

- The rest of the young men in Kmt were informally taught by their fathers, skills outside of arithmetic, writing, and reading (Sifuna & Otiende, 2006).

l. The fathers in Kmt were responsible for teaching their children piety, morality, and reverence for the per-Aa.

m. Mothers in Kmt were responsible for teaching young girls the *domestic arts*. The girls in royal families had opportunities to receive a more "formal" education suited to fit their life status.

DR. IVAN VAN SERTIMA

BRIEF AUTHOR BIO

- Born in Guyana, South America

- Lectured at more than 100 colleges in the U.S.

- Fmr. Prof. of Africana Studies – Rutgers University

- Author of *They Came Before Columbus*

- Other famous publications include *African Presence in Early Europe* & *African Presence in Early Asia*

- Was Founder & Editor – Journal of African Civilizations in 1979

Sources: journalofafricancivilizations.com/VanSertima

BLACKS IN SCIENCE: ANCIENT AND MODERN

MANUSCRIPT TYPE: Book

Main Points from the Text:

a. Kmt gave birth to the world's first doctors, whose skill was unparalleled in the ancient world.

b. The early Greeks associated the Kemetic multi-genius, Imhotep with their healing deity, known as Asclepios.

- Imhotep was known to the Greeks by the name Imouthes.

  • It is interesting to note that many medical historians, when discussing the many accomplishments and contributions of Imhotep, ignore and/or do not mention that Imhotep was a Black Afrikan man (Van Sertima, 1998).

c. Some scholars disagree and have stated that the world's first known physician does not belong to Imhotep but to Hesy-Re, who lived ca. 2600 B.C.E. However, Kemetic scholar-priest, Manetho, wrote that the son of Per-Aa Min (Menes to the Greeks), Per-Aa Djer (Athothis to the Greeks) was also a physician.

- Manetho also stated that Per-Aa Djer had written various texts on the topic of anatomy (Van Sertima, 1998).

- Hesy-Re was Chief of Dentists and Physicians in Kmt (Van Sertima, 1998).

- The reason some scholars disagree about Imhotep being a physician is because references of Imhotep as a physician did not appear until later in Kemetic history.

d. At one time, Athens, the Greek city-state, was importing Kemetic physicians.

- Other kingdoms in the Near East region did the same.

e. Homer also spoke on the medical knowledge of the Kemites:

   "... And in medical knowledge, Egypt leaves the rest of the world behind" (Van Sertima, 1998, p. 140).

f. The ancient Kemites were producing medical texts as far back as 5,000 years ago.

   - This sacred medical knowledge was passed on orally from the medical priests to their students, as this has long been a custom in Africa itself.

   - Kemetic medical priests also kept their best medical knowledge hidden or secret (Van Sertima, 1998).

g. The physicians in Kmt were taught and trained in the *Per Ankh* (House of Life).

   - The per ankh acted as a university where physicians completed their studies; it also acted as a: library, medical school, clinic, temple, and a seminary (Van Sertima, 1998).

h. Many of the Greek intellectuals, such as Thales, Pythagoras, and Plato were trained in the per ankhs of Kmt.

- Dr. George G. M. James (2001) provides a wealth of evidence in his work *Stolen Legacy*, showing that many of Greece's intellectuals went to Kmt to receive their training and education. The Greek desire was so strong to be associated with Kmt's education system that even those in Greece who never went to Kmt to get an education lied and said that they did anyhow.

- Within the Per Ankhs, there was no compartmentalization of subjects and fields that were being taught (Van Sertima, 1998).

- What is popularly known as religion, philosophy, science, astronomy, mathematics, music, and mdu nTr, were considered all part of the same family of knowledge. Aspects of each field could be found in others.

i. Kmt was the only known nation in antiquity that had physicians that specialized in specific areas (Van Sertima, 1998).

- During the Old Kingdom (2665 – 2160 B.C.E.), diseases affecting the various organs were being treated by specialists of those organs.

- At one point, the practice of specializing in a certain field was phased out. Not until the Ptolemaic Period (332 – 30 B.C.E.) did the practice of being a specialist become popular again in Kmt.

  - The reason for this new found popularity in being a specialist is attributed to their being a strong interest in the old Kemetic culture.

- The developments made by Kemetic physician-priests in the field of medicine were and remains unmatched.

j. Physicians in Kmt were "government employees", and healthcare was provided to everyone who needed it (a universal healthcare system).

k. Many of the medical papyri that still exist reveal that the Kemites had an understanding of the cardiovascular system some 4,500 years prior to that of physician, William Harvey M.D.'s "discovery" of circulation (Van Sertima, 1998).

- The Kemites were aware of the heart being the center of the cardiovascular system.

- Bestetti, Restini, and Couto (2014) wrote an article regarding the development of a structural and functional knowledge of the cardiovascular system and its relationship to the rest of the body (anatomophysiology) in Kmt.

  In their article, the authors had this to say:

"In ancient Egypt (3500 BC), the heart was considered the central element of a system of channels distributed throughout the body..."

The authors went further to say:

"...There was a clear notion that the peripheral pulse originated from the heartbeat ... and that pulse measurement could be performed using a clepsydra. The doctor perhaps compared the patient's pulse with his own..." (Bestetti, Restini, & Couto, 2014, p. 538).

- Reinaldo Bulgarelli Bestetti, Carolina Baraldi A. Restini, and Lucélio B. Couto have all written extensively in the field of cardiology and other areas of medicine, having appeared in over 200 journal articles.

1. Through intense, rigorous, and in-depth research, the Kemites were able to recognize the magnitude and severity of heart palpitations as well as arrhythmias (Van Sertima, 1998).

- Kemitic physicians talked about chest pains (angina pectoris), interruptions in one's heartbeat (arrhythmia), and unusually fast heart beats. Kemetic physicians were also produced a very clear cut definition of chest pains as a result of coronary heart disease in the following passage:

  > "If thou examinest a man for illness in his cardia and he has pains in his arms, in his breast, and on one side of his cardia... it is death threatening him" (Van Sertima, 1998, p. 142).

m. The Kemites also knew that too much blood that gathers in the heart and lungs was indeed pathological and is congruent with the condition known today as congestive heart failure.

n. Kemetic physicians also had knowledge of and names for the human brain and meninges (Van Sertima, 1998).

- Kemetic physicians had knowledge of the relationship that exists between the nervous system and voluntary movements.

o. The names for the ureters (which connect the kidneys and bladder) were known and named by the Kemites.

p. The Kemites possessed knowledge of neuro-anatomy that was every bit as detailed and advanced as modern knowledge on the subject (Van Sertima, 1998).

q. Kemetic physicians knew the genesis of paraplegia and paralysis as a result of injuries to the spinal cord.

r. Physicians also recognized traumatic beginnings of neurological problems: deafness, priapism, urinal incontinence, etc. (Van Sertima, 1998).

s. The Kemites had bonesetters, who were individuals who specialized in treating fractured bones and dislocations.

- These bone setting specialists had also developed a technique for effectively reducing fractured collarbones.

- This technique for reducing fractured bones was later used by Hippocrates.

GREAT BLACK LEADERS: ANCIENT AND MODERN

MANUSCRIPT TYPE: Book

Main Points from the Text:

a. Per-Aa Hatshepsut established a "science of rulership" that had been relatively unheard of in the ancient world at that time (Van Sertima, 1999, p. 15).

- The core of this new way of ruling involved a woman displaying traits that are considered masculine.

b. At the very beginning of the dynastic periods in Kmt, the science of medicine is already a fully formed discipline being practiced as a result of thousands of years of prior research and observation (Van Sertima, 1999).

- The Ebers and Edwin Smith papyri pre-date the construction of the pyramids.

- A fully defined medicine curriculum along with a large collection of medical literature was already in place at the beginning of Kmt's history.

c. One of the per-Aas from the First Dynasty in Kmt (ca. 3100 B.C.E.) was a renowned physician (Van Sertima, 1999).

d. Using the very first known calendar date of 4236 B.C.E., which is the likely beginning of dynastic history in Kmt, dates the genesis of Kemetic medicine back to at least 7000 B.C.E.

e. Once the Edwin Smith papyrus was translated in 1930, it was clear that Imhotep, not Hippocrates, was the first known "Father of Medicine."

- The Edwin Smith papyrus pre-dates Hippocrates by 2,500 years (Van Sertima, 1999).

f. Imhotep's father, Kanofer, was a very well-known and respected architect during his lifetime (Van Sertima, 1999).

EGYPT REVISITED

MANUSCRIPT TYPE: Book

Main Points from the Text:

a. Hippocrates never discussed pulse-taking techniques, whereas the Kemites did, and the technique can be found in the so-called Edwin Smith Papyrus (Van Sertima, 1999).

- So-called Hippocratic methods of setting clavicular (collarbone) fractures and dislocated jaws are virtually identical to Kemetic methods in the Edwin Smith papyrus.

b. The method for reducing dislocated jaws was first seen in the *Edwin Smith* papyrus (Van Sertima, 1999).

- The claim is often made that Alexandrian Greek, Herophilus, discovered diagnostic applications of taking a person's pulse.

- These diagnostic applications, such as pulse-taking and others, can be found in the Ebers and Edwin Smith papyri that came 3,500 years before Herophilus.

- Herophilus, along with another Alexandrian Greek scholar, Erasistratus, are once again given recognition for being "the first" to accomplish something that they did not.

This time it was outline the connections between the peripheral nerves and the central nervous system (CNS), which is also found in the Edwin Smith papyrus (Van Sertima, 1999).

Many of the so-called medical discoveries attributed to ancient Greek scholars they themselves did not discover. In fact, several of the so-called Greek medical miracles were simply rediscoveries of what Kemetic physicians had already worked tirelessly to find out.

c. The sudden surge in Greek medicine in Alexandria can be contributed to a single source; the gathering of all of the then extant scientific papyri of the Kemites.

d. What are thought to be the first anatomical descriptions on record were found in Kmt.

- Over 200 anatomical parts have been found in existing Kemetic medical texts (Van Sertima, 1999). Some of them are:

    - *Djnnt* or jenet – Cranium

    - *Gma* or gema – Temporal bone

    - *Shrt* or sheret – Nostril

DR. THEOPHILE OBENGA

BRIEF AUTHOR BIO

- Assisted in writing the *General History of Africa* series of books

- Authored works in French, such *Le Zaire, Civilisations traditionnelles et Culture moderne*

- Dir. & Chief Editor of the Ankh journal

- Member of French Association of Egyptologists (Société Française D'Egyptologie)

- Helped to defend Egypt as being part of Africa; its history/culture at the 1974 Cairo UNESCO Symposium

---

Sources: africana.sfsu.edu/people/faculty/theophile-j-obenga

ANCIENT EGYPT

&

BLACK AFRICA

MANUSCRIPT TYPE: Book

Main Points from the Text:

a. Several philosophical works were produced during the
time of the per-Aas in Kmt. The following is a
breakdown from the text (Obenga, 1992):

- Old Kingdom (ca. 2815 – 2400 B.C.E.)

  - The Pyramid Texts

  - Teachings or Wisdoms or Instructions

  - Teachings of Imhotep

  - Teachings of Hordjedef

- Teachings for Kagemni

- Teachings of Ptah-hotep

- Teachings of Kaires

- First Intermediate Period (Nineth – Eleventh Dynasties ca. 2300 – 2050 B.C.E.)

  - Admonitions of an Egyptian Sage (Ipuwer's prophecies)

  - Dialogue of a Desperate Person and His Ba (soul)

  - The Teachings for King Merikare

  - Songs of the Harpist

  - Tales of the Oasian

- Middle Kingdom (ca. 2000 – 1800 B.C.E.)

  - The Teaching of Amenemhat to his son Senusret (Sesostris to the Greeks)

  - Satire of Trades

  - Tales of the Westcar Papyrus

- The Coffin Texts

- New Kindom (ca. 1590 – 1085 B.C.E.)

  - The Book of Coming Forth by Day (Book of the Dead)

  - The Great Hymn to the Aton

  - The Wisdom of Ani

  - The Teachings of Amenemope

- Late Period (Twenty-First – Thirtieth Dynasties ca. 1000 – 332 B.C.E.)

  - Inscriptions from the Tomb of Ankhefenkhons (Petosiris to the Greeks)

* Brief descriptions of each text listed above can be found on pages 31 – 35.

b. Philosophy was first defined during the reign of Per-Aa Mentuhotep (Obenga, 1992).

- Philosophy is explained as (educated) guesses regarding the fate and circumstances of humanity.

Prior to the modern usage and understanding of the term, philosophy referred to all human knowledge. The greatest purpose of philosophy was for humans to obtain wisdom (what the Greeks called *Sophia*).

- The term philosophy was a strange and foreign word to the Greeks, thus indicating that it could not have originated in Greece.

c. Isocrates identified Kmt as the place where medicine and of the philosophy for the well-being of one's soul originated (Isocrates, 1928; Obenga, 1992).

d. For hundreds of years, Kmt had a dominating influence on Greece in the areas of geometry, philosophy, medicine, mathematics, and astronomy. The following examples speak to the dominance of Kemetic influence on ancient Greece and Greek thinkers (Obenga, 1992).

- Philosopher and mathematician, Thales, studied in Kmt under the only known master teachers he had during his lifetime.

- Solon, a lawmaker from Athens, was the student of scholarly priest Sanchis/Sonchis of Sau (Sais to the Greeks) in Kmt.

- Samos native and scholar, Pythagoras, studied for about twenty-two years in the Kemetic city of Men-nefer (Memphis to the Greeks), Waset (Thebes to the Greeks), and On (Heliopolis to the Greeks).

  - Isocrates raised in his writing referring to Pythagoras:

    "He came to Egypt, and became the disciple of the people there; he was the first to bring philosophy to Greece" (Isocrates, 1928, p. 28).

  - It should be noted that scholars today agree that Thales is thought to be the first to do this, not Pythagoras.

- Anaxagoras, a philosopher from Clazomenae (modern day Klazomenai, Turkey), traveled to Kmt to master a more precise science for studying nature.

- Philosopher and writer, Pherecydes of Syros, journeyed to Kmt where he was taught theology among other sciences.

- Philosopher, Democritus, studied astronomy and geometry for five years in Kmt under his master teacher, Pammenes of Men-nefer.

- Plato studied in Kmt with at least two known master teachers; Khnuphis at Men-nefer and SeKnuphis at On.

e. Aristotle boasted that Kmt was the cradle of mathematics. He asserted the following:

"So the mathematical arts were first, formed, constituted only in Egypt" (Aristotle, 1933, p. 981 b 23).

- The Greeks, Aristotle included, took pride in having been educated in Kmt.

f. Thales of Miletus, mathematician and philosopher, who is believed to be the founder of wisdom in

Europe, had no other known teachers except those in Kmt.

g. It is unclear how long exactly Thales spent in Kmt receiving his education. Second century philosopher Aetius proclaimed that Thales studied for several years in Kmt and returned to Miletus as an elder (Obenga, 2015; 1992). Pythagoras completed his education in Kmt after studying for twenty-two years under Kemetic scholarly priests.

AFRICAN PHILOSOPHY: THE PHARAONIC PERIOD: 2780 – 330 BC

MANUSCRIPT TYPE: Book

Main Points from the Text:

a. The profession of teacher in ancient Kmt was highly respected and revered.

■ An ancient Kemetic scholar named Neb-Maa-Re Nakht wrote of respect given to teachers in the Papyrus Lansing. This text was from the twentieth dynasty (ca. 1567 – 1085 B.C.E.) (Obenga, 2004).

b. Several institutions of learning existed for boys seeking to enter the profession of scribe.

- The boys who chose this area of study had to be virgins, and thus, had not yet gone through "puberty" – See the Papyrus Lansing.

c. Plato, in his *The Laws*, very clearly praised the Kemetic education system, going as far as to recommend it as a model for all Athenian students (Obenga, 2004).

d. During the nineteenth and twentieth dynasties, the standard or traditional education system was called the *Great Eternal Teaching System* (Obenga, 2004).

- In this system, sons received training from their expert fathers.

e. Public education was commonplace in Kmt from the beginning of the Middle Kingdom period (ca. 2052 – 1778 B.C.E.).

f. Before the creation of so-called public schools, education was homeschooling, with the responsibility of educating the children falling completely to the parents.

- It was the responsibility of the parents to ensure that their children learned all of the social ethics of society.

g. There was a textbook thought to exist by the name of *Kemit*, which was used to teach reading and writing (Obenga, 2004).

h. Teachers disciplined students who "stepped out of line" and misbehaved.

- In the Papyrus Lansing, a student is quoted as saying *"Because you beat me on the back, your teaching entered my ears"* (Obenga, 2004, p.570).

i. The Kemetic writing system was not an invention of nor was it borrowed from Mesopotamia. It was locally developed by the ancient Kemites

- The mdu nTr was stocked with ideograms, phonograms, materials to write on, and scribal instruments.

j. By the start of the second millennia B.C.E., the mdu nTr contained around 700 signs (Obenga, 2004).

  - Under Greek and Roman domination, additional signs were added, bringing the total to over 5,000 signs that were used during the Ptolemaic period (ca. 332 – 30 B.C.E.).

  - This type of communication is still present today in the form of signs and alerts that represent an object or an idea (ideograms), and can be seen in one's town (e.g. a sign for slippery streets).

k. Symbols representing sounds (phonograms) were developed due to the Kemites realizing that the ideograms alone were not enough to clearly communicate certain ideas, feelings, and so forth.

- There were approximately 150 phonographic symbols in the mdu nTr (Obenga, 2004).

l. mdu nTr was developed to be written four different ways (Obenga, 2004):

  - Horizontally, from left to right

  - Horizontally, from right to left

  - Vertically, from right to left

  - Vertically, from left to right

- The writing direction of each column was always downward.

m. Two other known cursive forms of the mdu nTr were developed; Hieratic and Demotic (Obenga, 2004).

- Earliest known documents with Hieratic writing date back to the First Dynasty period (ca. 3100 B.C.E.).

- Around the end of the seventh century B.C.E., Demotic (popular writing) was developed and being used as a true common form of writing.

- Plotinus, a Greek philosopher born in Lower Kmt, declared that the mdu nTr was a science and body of wisdom.

n. More than 2,500 years ago, the Kemites were already investigating our beginnings and meaning of existence, as well as the issue of knowledge of the world and cosmos.

o. The Inscription of Shabaka, shows that Kemetic philosopher-priests were already figuring out the workings of creation in Kmt; specifically in this example, Ineb-hedj/Men-nefer (Memphis).

- An Old Kingdom text (ca. 2780 – 2260 B.C.E.) was inscribed in a large granite stele by order of the Per-Aa Shabaka, going back to the per-Aanic origins of civilization.

To quote Dr. Obenga:

"In other words, over 2,000 years before Thales, pharaonic Egypt produced a magnificent philosophy ... an ordered conception of life, phrased in language which suggests that the tradition already had several centuries of maturity behind it by then" (Obenga, 2004, p. 86).

p. The Kemites also engaged in mapmaking and showed an expert understanding of the physical history of the earth (geology), as evidenced by the Gold Mines map of Wadi Hammamat or Gold Mines Papyrus.

q. Orthogonal projection (representation of 3D objects in a 2-D space) was invented by the Kemites circa 1100 B.C.E. (Obenga, 2004).

r. The Kemites calculated the size of the earth.

- They knew that the earth is a sphere due to tracking the shadows left by sunlight upon the earth.

s. Kemetic scientists had calculated the variations in the length of days and night at various times of the year.

t. Fifth century Latin writer, Macrobius, proclaimed that Kemetic scholars knew of Mercury and Venus' existence and of their orbiting the sun.

- Kemetic scholars called Mercury the "Red Heru (Horus)" (Obenga, 2004).

u. Per-Aanic Kmt left many different calendars behind (Obenga, 2004):

- (1) Diagonal calendars of the Middle Kingdom period (ca. 2060 – 1785 B.C.E.). (2) So-called Louvre calendar. (3) A time count based on a new type of water-powered clock that was built at the beginning of the eighteenth dynastic period (ca. 1554 B.C.E.). (4) 'Star tables' of the twentieth dynastic period (ca. 1187 B.C.E.). (5) A calendar that lists lucky and unlucky days written on the verso side of a Ramesside papyrus in Cairo.

v. Speaking of chemistry, Kemetic scientists had a very precise knowledge of acids.

- Some of their insights and processes that were developed are still being used. An example being the Gobelin tapestry workshop of the seventeenth century (Obenga, 2004).

- Chemical analyses of fabrics found in ancient Kemetic tombs revealed that the red tincture used to dye them was derived from a rose, *Carthamus tinctorius.*

- A thorough and in-depth investigation of the history of textiles should start with per-Aanic Kmt, at the start of the Old Kingdom period.

w. Kemetic physicians were very knowledgeable when it came to dissection. Let us consider the following case of lockjaw described by a Kemetic physician in the Edwin Smith Papyrus:

"...his lower jawbone is drawn tight means that there is a cramp in the muscles at the tip of that part of his lower jawbone joined to his temporal bone, at the end of his jaw, which is locked..." (Obenga, 2004, p. 415).

x. Kemetic physicians also wrote medical treatises on individuals with brain damage, lesions on their spinal column, concussions, and other ailments.

- There was a treatise called *The Book of Wounds*, which was a compilation of 48 different surgical case studies done by Kemetic physicians (Obenga, 2004).

- Two types of injuries and/or lesion were analyzed:

  - Surface cuts

  - Bone and joint lesions

y. Kemetic physicians never saw illnesses as punishments for any type of so-called sin(s) that one may have committed.

z. Some of the anatomical terms used in Kmt include:

- *wXdw* or ukhedu – Sensation of pain

- *wpt* or upet – Top of one's skull

- *mt* or met – Nerves, ligaments, tendons, etc.

- *inm* or inem – Color or shade of one's epidermis (skin)

- *mndj* or menej – A human breast

- *ntnt* or netenet – The meninges covering of the brain and spinal cord.

- *wAb* or uab – A tooth socket (Obenga, 2015, p. 388).

- *kAt* or kat – The human vagina.

* See p. 383 for a larger list of anatomical terms that Kemetic physicians used (Obenga, 2004).

aa. The so-called Berlin Papyrus (ca. 1305 – 1205 B.C.E.) exposed the fact that Kemetic medical professionals pioneered the process of using the urine of pregnant women to signal a pregnancy.

- The Kemites also utilized the urine of a pregnant woman in predicting the sex of a child before birth.

This method included the usage of one bag of barley and one bag of wheat.

bb. Another equally prominent method used by the Kemites to indicate if a woman was pregnant or not was the utilization of garlic (Obenga, 2004).

- This particular pregnancy detection method was recorded in the so-called Kahoun Papyrus written during the middle of the twelfth dynasty (ca. 1850 B.C.E.), and later in the so-called Carlsberg Papyrus during the nineteenth or possibly twentieth dynasty (ca. 1200 B.C.E.).

- Hippocrates saw fit to copy this usage of garlic in Greece to figure out whether or not a woman would become pregnant.

AFRICAN PHILOSOPHY

MANUSCRIPT TYPE: Book

Main Points from the Text:

a. The texts produced by Imhotep (2660 B.C.E.), Kagemni, and Ptahotep (2600 B.C.E.), as well as the texts found within the pyramids (beginning in 2350 B.C.E.) revealed the first known ethical, philosophical, and metaphysical texts to be documented in Africa.

- Philosophy was science and science was philosophy in Kmt (Obenga, 2015, p. 19).

b. The astronomer priests of Inw (Iunu/On) (Heliopolis to the Greeks) identified the solar year of 365 days based on the path of the sun through the heavens.

c. In antiquity, the journey that Mercury and Venus took around the sun was labeled the 'Egyptian System' (Obenga, 2015).

- The 'Egyptian System' referred to a sequence of movements in the universe and the way the two planets mentioned revolve around our sun, at times being positioned behind the sun.

d. Macrobius is cited as saying:

   "Plato followed the Egyptians, the parents of all sciences, who placed the sun between the moon and Mercury" (Obenga, 2015, p. 39).

e. Imhotep, having designed the Step Pyramid at Saqqara, became the first known person to build with stone.

   - Imhotep was also a high priest, being well versed in Kemetic spirituality, and the true father of medicine.

f. Peseshet was the earliest known woman to become a doctor in recorded history.

   - She carried the titles *imyt-r-swnwwt*, (the lady director of lady physicians), and *imyt-r-hwt-ka*, (the lady director of lady soul-priestesses) (Obenga, 2015).

g. There were specialist physicians assigned to the per-Aa and the royal family.

- Swnw-irty-per-aa, meaning *physician of the eyes of the Great House*, was the royal optometrist (Obenga, 2015).

h. Thales, the first known Greek philosopher, received an education and training within Kmt's educational system.

- There are at least a half a dozen prominent Greek writers who corroborate this fact, such as: Diogenes Laertius, Plato, Aetius, Proclus, Iamblichus, and Plutarch, and so on.

- Thales strongly recommended to Pythagoras that he go to Kmt to receive an education (Obenga, 2015).

AFRICA:
THE CRADLE OF WRITING

MANUSCRIPT TYPE: Research Article

Main Points from the Text:

a. Sanchuniathon's (san-choo-nye-uh-thun) was an author of Phoenician descent. He explicitly stated in his work, *Sanchuniathon's Book*, that writing was invented in Kmt by the Kemites (Obenga, 1999).

b. In *Phaedrus* (2005), Socrates points out that systems of writing were first invented in Kmt, due to the divine manifestation Djhuti/Tehuti (Thoth to the Greeks).

c. Most of the glyphs from Crete were taken from the Kemetic system of writing.

 * See the work titled *Scripta Minoa* by Arthur Evans.

d. Egyptologist and former Director of the German Archaeological Institute in Cairo, Dr. Gunther Dreyer found more than 200 hundred ancient ivory written texts in Aabdju (Abydos). These texts were determined to be older than the earliest Sumerian writings.

- There are researchers now who put the invention of the Sumerian script at least 3400 B.C.E.as well, with others seeming to suggest that writing developed simultaneously in both Kmt and Sumer.

e. The chronology of writing according to the article (Obenga, 1999, p. 88):

- Kemetic system of writing – 3400 B.C.E.

- Sumerian system of writing – 3060 B.C.E.

- Chinese system of writing – 1766 B.C.E.

- Mayan system of writing – 500 B.C.E.

DR. CHARLES S. FINCH III

BRIEF AUTHOR BIO

- Conducted frequent healing ceremonies in Senegal

- Lectured extensively in locations, such as the U.S., Egypt, Senegal, Jamaica

- Wrote for the Journal of African Civilizations

- Fmr. Asst. Dir. of International Health – Morehouse School of Medicine

- Has published a dozen or more articles since 1982

- Graduate of Yale & Jefferson Medical College

Sources: charlessfinch.com/bio.html

ECHOES OF THE OLD DARKLAND: THEMES FROM THE AFRICAN EDEN

MANUSCRIPT TYPE: Book

Main Points from the Text:

a. Some of the oldest known pictographic writing was being used in Kmt by 4200 B.C.E.

  - In Nubia, pictographic writing was in use approximately 300 years earlier than in Kmt (Finch, 2011).

b. It may have been the goddess Sesheta who oversaw the early development of writing in ancient Kmt.

- Sesheta is the female counterpart of Djhuti/Tehuti (Thoth to the Greeks), representing reading, writing, arithmetic, and architecture.

- The attributes of Sesheta are a strong implication that the roots of writing may have started with Afrikan women (Finch, 2011).

c. The Kemites were masters of chronology as shown by their discovery of the Great Year and creation of the calendar.

- In 1823, the French astronomer Jean-Baptiste Biot was the first modern astronomer to recognize that the Kemites had discovered the *Procession* or the *Great Year* (Finch, 2011).

- English scientist and astronomer Norman Lockyer also corroborated these findings.

- Austrian American mathematician and historian of science Otto Neugebauer was often reluctant to give credit to the Kemites for their scientific and educational achievements.

- Neugebauer was forced to admit that there had never been a more flawless example of a calendar than the one developed by the Kemites.

- English poet and author Gerald Massey was convinced that the Kemites discovered the Great Year as far back as 39,000 years ago.

d. The ancient Kemites were guided by both natural and cosmic cycles.

- These cycles are the closest thing to a bona fide calendar that valid anywhere on earth.

e. Kemetic scientists developed a conventional calendar consisting of 360 days (Finch, 2011).

- It is not by chance that the number of days in the conventional calendar matches the number of degrees in a geometric circle.

f. Kemetic astronomers were well aware of the earth being in the shape of a sphere, and explained its oval-shaped route around the sun.

g. Latin writer Martianus Capella proclaimed that the Kemites had been refining the science of astronomy for a period of at least 40,000 years.

THE STAR OF DEEP BEGINNINGS: THE GENESIS OF AFRICAN SCIENCE AND TECHNOLOGY

MANUSCRIPT TYPE: Book

Main Points from the Text:

a. 4,000 years ago in Kmt, there was a unity between science and knowledge.

- *tp-hsb n hat m khat nbt rekh ntt snkt shtat nbt* – refers to the correct method of investigating all things in order to know all that exists, each mystery and every secret (Finch, 2007).

- This is an evocation of the domain and purpose of mathematics.

  - This phrase was meant to invoke the rigor, precision, and methods of Kemetic science.

b. The Rhind papyrus infers that Kemetic mathematics can shed light on answers to the question *What is the nature of existence?* (Finch, 2007).

c. Efficient mining activities were being conducted in Kmt and in the Sinai area.

  - It is indicative of the Kemites possessing mining technology and a knowledge of its use.

  - The amount of ore that was mined in the Hapi (Nile) Valley during the dynastic epoch was just about equal to that of the rest of the world up to the beginning of the nineteenth century (Finch, 2007).

d. What are thought to be the first copper smelting furnaces in Kmt were developed in the Sinai area.

- Copper was one of and perhaps the very oldest metal used by humans; the beginnings of which date back to at least 10,000 B.C.E. (Finch, 2007).

- The process of annealing copper was also known in Kmt.

  - Annealing refers to making copper more malleable without compromising hardness, which was already known in the pre-dynastic epoch.

- Traces of arsenic were also known to be present in the copper found in Kmt.

  - William Flinders-Petrie was of the opinion that the Kemites were well aware that arsenical copper ore yielded a greater hardness (Finch, 2007).

- The casting of copper was developed in pre-dynastic times but by the dynastic period, the process was perfected.

e. Iron-working was a trade that was developed and learned in pre-dynastic times, and was associated with Heru (Horus) himself.

f. There was number system in Kmt, which was essentially a decimal system with fifteen number characters (Finch, 2007).

- Numeral characters one through nine were represented by tally marks.

- Powers of 10, up to 1,000,000, were represented by mdu nTr.

g. For daily accounting and calculations, the Kemites utilized a shortened and semi-cursive style of Hieratic.

h. Out of the four principal arithmetic operations, both multiplication and division were easily done using the mdu nTr number system (Finch, 2007).

- It remains unknown today just how the Kemites performed addition and subtraction tasks that they did perform with large numbers.

- There are historians who are convinced that Kemetic scholars used addition and subtraction tables that allow them to read off the answers as they needed them.

i. Kemetic scholars had a very interesting way of multiplying and doubling. One number would be the multiplier and the other, the multiplicand (Finch, 2007).

  - A multiplicand is a number that will be multiplied by another number.

j. The Kemites developed what is referred to as a 'unit fraction' system.

  - A unit fraction system is one that, with a single exception, all fractions had to be expressed with

  - The two-thirds fraction is a very unique fraction in Kemetic mathematics.

    • This fraction is used so often in both multiplication and division that some mathematics historians are of the belief that Kemetic scholars had a two-thirds fractions table. Gillings (1982) says that the two-thirds table would be good enough and explained that:

> "... for all the scribes' needs, and extended up to 100, it would enable them to find 2/3 of any number, integral, or fractional, because multiplication and division by 10 was a commonplace operation with them" (Finch, 2007, p. 66; Gillings, 1982, p. 27).

k. The Kemites also developed music and harmonics.

- Kemetic musicians could produce a variety of perfect melodies by playing the strings of the fingerboard a specific way.

  - This technique can be seen in modern day violinist and guitarists.

- Traveler, writer, and Egyptologist Gardner Wilkinson pointed out the following:

"It appears ... that music was studied by the Egyptian priests with other views than that of affording pleasure and entertainment, the same science being borrowed by Pythagoras from Egypt..." (Finch, 2007, p. 69-70; Wilkinson, 1878, p. 444).

l. It was in Kmt that Pythagoras studied the musical formulas (which he is famous for) that produced theories that connected numbers and harmony.

m. From the 1930s to the 1960s, Austrian born Mathematician Otto Neugebauer's attitude and beliefs about Kemetic mathematics can be summed up in the following quotes:

> *"The role of Egyptian mathematics is probably best described as a retarding force upon numerical procedures..."*

And...

"Ancient science was the product of a very few men; and these few happened not to be Egyptians..." (Finch, 2007, p. 78; Neugebauer, 1969, p. 80).

- English Egyptologist, Thomas Eric Peet, and American Professor of Mathematics, Morris Kline echoed similar attitudes to Neugebauer's.

- Kline had the following to say:

  "The mathematics of the Egyptians... is the scrawling of children just learning how to write, as opposed to great literature..." (Finch, 2007, p. 80; Kline, 1963, p. 14).

- Professor Richard Gillings was one of the few unprejudiced historians, and often defended Kemetic mathematics.

n. Ancient writers, such as Herodotus, Diodorus, and Clement often explicitly admitted where most if not all Greek mathematicians were trained; Kmt.

DR. CHEIKH ANTA DIOP

Brief Author Bio

- Assisted in forming the first Pan-African Student Congress in Paris

- Founded a radiocarbon dating lab - University of Dakar

- Was Prof. of Ancient Hist. –University of Dakar

- Received Ph.D. from University of Sorbonne

- Also authored: *The African Origins of Civilization: Myth or Reality* & *The Cultural Unity of Black Africa*

Sources:

radiocarbone2015.ucad.sn/index.php/presentation/le-parrain-de-l-ifan-chaikh-anta-diop

blackpast.org/global-african-history/diop-cheikh-anta-1923-1986/

CIVILIZATION OR BARBARISM: AN AUTHENTIC ANTHROPOLOGY

MANUSCRIPT TYPE: Book

Main Points from the Text:

a. Since the publishing of the Papyrus Moscow, it was revealed that the Kemites had created the formulae for the area of a sphere $(S = 4\pi R^2)$ 2,000 years before Archimedes (Diop, 1991).

■ Russian Orientalist and historian V. V. Struve put forth an enormous effort to figure out the approach of Kemetic mathematics.

b. The Rhind Papyrus, which was published by T. Eric Peet revealed that the Kemites had a precise knowledge of the volume of a cylinder ($V = \pi R^2 h$).

c. The ancient Kemites also knew the area of a circle ($S = \pi R^2$), using a π value of 3.16, and the volume of a truncated pyramid ($V = h/3\,(a^2 + ab + b^2)$) (Diop, 1991).

d. Eudoxus and Plato were former students of the Kemetic priests at On (Heliopolis).

- The Kemites were already working with mathematical formulae 2,000 years before the birth of both Eudoxus and Plato. Kemetic scholars have not received the credit deserved for the formulae shown in exercise 14 of the so-called Moscow Papyrus. The same is true of exercises 56, 57, 58, 59, and 60 of the so-called Rhind Papyrus. The credit for such formulae often mistakenly goes to Greek scholars.

e. The Kemites had already solved the problem of the equilibrium of the lever during the building of the pyramids (ca. 2600 B.C.E.) (Diop, 1991).

- The equilibrium of the lever was a problem that Archimedes also addressed in a treatise he wrote some 2,000 years after the Kemites dealt with this problem.

- In order for a stone weighing five-million tons to be lifted to a height of 148 meters; one would need to possess a precise knowledge of mechanics and the leverage theory.

f. V. V. Struve wrote the following:

"Also we must admit that in mechanics the Egyptians had more knowledge than we wanted to believe... The Egyptian plans are as correct as those of modern engineers..." (Diop, 1991, p. 243).

g. The Kemites were the creators of the scale. The scale was the first known exact and rigid scientific utilization of the leverage theory.

h. Problem 53 of the Rhind Papyrus of Kmt brings to light the Kemetic geometric theorem that Thales borrowed his theorem from. Thales is too often mistakenly credited with discovering this theorem that clearly was in existence 1,700 years before he was born.

i. P.H. Michel was cited as saying the following regarding the mathematical theorem that Pythagoras incorrectly receives credit for:

"Whether stated or not by Pythagoras himself,... the connection... had, furthermore, already been known for a long time by the Egyptians and the Babylonians, who had verified it in certain cases..." (Diop, 1991, p.246).

j. V. V. Struve is quoted as stating the following about Kemetic science:

"The Papyrus Moscow...confirms ... statements of Greek writers on the mathematical knowledge of the Egyptian scholars. We... no longer have... reason to reject the affirmations of the Greek writers according to whom the Egyptians were... masters ... in geometry" (Diop, 1991, p. 248).

k. V. V. Struve constantly proclaimed that the brain was talked about in the Edwin Smith Papyrus. He also added that the term for the brain was unknown in all other scientific languages in the East of that time.

- The Kemetic author of the Edwin Smith Papyrus already knew of how the body is dependent on the brain.

l. According to the Greek tradition, geometry came to Hellas from Kmt; not Babylonia.

m. The Kemites were the sole originators and developers of the calendar, which overall remained unchanged to this day.

- The Kemetic year was separated into 36 decades, or 10-day time periods, for a total of 360 divisions or degrees. Each 10-day period was controlled by a constellation (Diop, 1991).

n. Over and over again one finds Theophrastus, Dioscorides, and Galen all pointing out the prescriptions that they got from the Kemetic physicians (Diop, 1991).

   - Galen stated that they learned these prescriptions by reading through the medical texts within the library of the Temple of Imhotep at Ineb-hedj/Men-nefer (Memphis).

o. Kemetic physicians often used psychological techniques in their treatments. These psychological techniques included the use of 'spells' and were part of magical formulas. The 'spells' were effective all on their own, and did not always require the aid of medicinal drugs.

- There were times though; when the magical formulas were buttressed by a drug to increase its effectiveness.

p. Over time, Kemetic physicians replaced magical formulas with medical treatments (Diop, 1991).

q. The root of the term chemistry is of Kemetic origin, coming from the word Kemit; pointing at the lengthy cooking process and distillations that were so commonplace in Kemetic labs.

- French chemist Claude Louis Berthollet greatly respected Kemetic knowledge of chemistry (Diop, 1991).

r. In the development of Kemetic philosophical thought, the concept of the being was comprised of four principles (Diop, 1991, p. 312):

- *Zed* or *Khet* (decomposes after death)

- The *Ba* (the body's corporeal soul)

- The being's shadow

- The *Ka* (immortal essence or life force that rejoins the divinity after one dies).

s. The location and direction of the monuments throughout Kmt confirms the conclusion that an intelligent astronomical science existed there.

  - Kemetic scientists had developed a scientific way of determining true north.

t. Kemetic scholars had a fully developed cosmogony (origin and development story of the universe) in place at a time before the Greeks and when Chinese and Hindu philosophies had no meaning (Diop, 1991).

  - There were three systems of Kemetic cosmogony:

  - Hermopolitan, Heliopolitan, Theban.

DR. MOLEFI ASANTE

BRIEF AUTHOR BIO

- Appeared in numerous movies, such as 500 Years Later

- Co-founder of the Journal of Black Studies

- Founded the theory of Afrocentricity

- Prof. & Chair – Dept. African-American Studies – Temple University

- Authored 77 books, such as *The History of Africa Second Ed.* & *The Encyclopedia of African Religion*

Sources: asante.net/biography/

THE EGYPTIAN PHILOSOPHERS: ANCIENT AFRICAN VOICES FROM IMHOTEP TO AKHENATEN

MANUSCRIPT TYPE: Book

Main Points from the Text:

a. Works produced by the African thinkers of antiquity were referred to as *seboyet*; a term translated as instruction(s) or wisdom (Asante, 2000).

- The term *seboyet* likely originated during the Old Kingdom period in Kmt (ca. 2665 – 2160 B.C.E.).

b. The Greeks began to call African intellectuals and scholars *physiologoi* (observers of the nature of things or nature philosophers).

c. From the system of observation that the African intellectuals exhibited sprang:

  - Astronomy, measurement, the calendar, and medicine (Asante, 2000).

d. Thales was a student in Kmt for such a long period of time that he was able to obtain a precise knowledge of mathematics, geometry, philosophy, basics of measuring land, and triangulation.

e. The following is a list of Black African scholars and philosophers, whom are referred to as thinkers. The following list is **NOT** a complete one (Asante, 2000, p. xiii):

  - Imhotep (ca. 2700 B.C.E.)

Earliest known person in human history to explore and handle the concepts of space, time, volume, nature of disease, and so forth, and the questions surrounding them.

- Ptahhotep (ca. 2414 B.C.E.)

  Held the belief that humanity must develop a peaceful bond and live harmoniously with nature. Ptahhotep was the earliest known person to consider questions of ethics concerning aging.

- Kagemni (ca. 2300 B.C.E.)

  Kagemni is often thought of as the first known teacher of ethics. Kagemni also desired to see humanity live upright and just lives; performing good deeds in order to become good people, rather than for personal gain alone.

- Merikare (ca. 1990 B.C.E.)

Often called the "philosopher of communication",
Merikare often taught the values of *mdu nfr* (good
speech) and common sense in our dealings with
others.

- Sehotepibre (ca. 1991 B.C.E.)

  Referred to as the 'Loyalist,' Sehotepibre was one of
  the earliest philosophers of Kmt to focus on
  nationalism, and stressed the importance of loyalty
  and being dedicated to the per-Aa.

- Amenemhat (ca. 1991 B.C.E.)

  Amenemhat was quite often labeled as a
  "cautionary philosopher." He was the first known
  person to convey doubts about those closest to you;
  urging others to be wary of those nearest to them.

- Amenhotep, son of Hapu (ca. 1400 B.C.E.)

  After Imhotep, Amenhotep, son of Hapu was one
  of the most respected and honored philosophers in

Kmt. Due to his dedication to teaching the principles of maAt, he was the only other teacher in Kmt besides Imhotep to be worshipped as a manifestation of the Creator.

- Duauf (ca. 1340 B.C.E.)

  Duauf's philosophy focused on societal codes according to which one should live their life; this included urging the youth of Kmt to develop a love of reading books.

- Akhenaton (ca. 1300 B.C.E.)

  Often mistakenly referred to as the father of Monotheism, Akhenaton chose Aton as the single true manifestation of the Creator to worship. This decision to install the Aton priesthood and the worship of Aton caused major social upheaval in Kmt.

- Amen-em-ipet (Amenemope) (ca. 1290 B.C.E.)

Amen-em-ipet was known to strongly advocate for the philosophy of good manners, etiquette, and overall success in life. Amen-em-ipet viewed humans being without experience and wisdom unless there were proverbs or wise sayings to guide them.

f. It was from the priests of Kmt that one first finds the idea that humans respond to varying levels of consciousness.

g. Some of the earliest ideas to surface in Kmt were ankh, seneb, djed, heheh, neter, and meri; all of which were taught and repeated throughout Kmt (Asante, 2000).

- *Ankh* – Life and existence.

- *Seneb* – Wellness and health

- *Djed* – Stability

- *Heheh* – Eternity

- *Neter* – Divine, deity; nature.

- *Meri* – Beloved or love

h. The three seasons of Akhit (Inundation/Flood), Peret/Perit (Emergence), and Shemu (Harvest or Drought) supported the development of science very early on in Kmt (Asante, 2000).

  - Every year in June, the Hapi (Nile) would flood (Akhit)

  - The Hapi waters reached their peak and begin to recede (Peret/Perit)

    - During Peret/Perit, there would be the harvesting of crops, and a drought would persist until the next flooding of the Hapi.

i. Books in the form of papyri were very plentiful throughout Kmt.

- While not everyone could read, Kemetic society used methods to convey images and ideas were needed to express the Kemetic understanding of creation at temples, and so forth. Therefore, the strong encouragement to read was very likely meant to spark and promote widespread literacy.

THE HISTORY OF AFRICA: THE QUEST FOR ETERNAL HARMONY

MANUSCRIPT TYPE: Book

Main Points from the Text:

a. Kemetic lawyers/jurists, such as Ptahhotep, were the founders of the science of international law.

- Kemetic lawyers/jurists were taught and taught others how to draft treaties, like those drafted and used between African and Western Asian nations.

- Lawyer and educator Jeremy I. Levitt has done extensive work in the area of law. He reported the following conclusions regarding international law (Asante, 2019):

- Seventeenth century lawyer Hugo Grotius and eighteenth century international lawyer Emer de Vattel were not the founding fathers of international law.

- The Treaty of Westphalia was based in large part on ideas that originated in Africa.

- Kemetic jurisprudence stands at the beginning of Western jurisprudence.

- Levitt asked the intriguing question:

  "Could the modern African state benefit from ancient African knowledge and approaches to governance, justice, and development?" (Levitt, 2015, p. 2)

b. Civil servants in Kmt were mostly comprised of: tax collectors and seshu (scribes) (Asante, 2019).

- Tax collectors in Kmt used the Hapi (Nile) to gather information for tax purposes.

c. Time keeping was another skill that was needed to maintain Kmt as a nation.

- By observing the skies and the Hapi, Kemetic scientists were able to perfect keeping time without digital tools.

- Many of the Kemetic scientists would climb to the top of the temples at night to observe the skies and stars; doing so all night.

d. The Kemites had three calendar seasons (Asante, 2019, p. 36):

- Months of Akhet (Inundation)

  - Tehuti, Phaophi, Aithir, Choiak

- Months of Peret (Emergence)

  - Tobi, Mechir, Phamenoth, Pharmuthi

- Months of Shemu (Planting)

- Pakhonsu, Payni, Epiphi, Mesore

e. Writing was reported to have originated in Kmt much earlier than Mesopotamia.

- This claim is supported by a discovery by Gunter Dreyer, which dates writing in Kmt back to at least 3400 B.C.E. (Asante, 2019). Dreyer was an Egyptologist for the German Archaeological Institute.

  - The earliest examples of writing in Mesopotamia are dated at between 3200 and 3000 B.C.E.

f. The first known examples of architectural and masonry skills were found in Kmt with the construction of the Step Pyramid of Saqqara.

g. Philosophy originated in Kmt. Many different factors brought this development about (Asante, 2019).

- There was a pressing need to explain the challenges of the universe in ways that were congruent and matched the spiritual ideas of the Kemetic people.

h. Some of the most important philosophers in Kmt's history were (Asante, 2019, p. 45):

- Imhotep, Merikare, Sehotipibre, Amenemhat, Amenhotep son of Hapu, Duauf, and Akhenaton.

i. The earliest known books of mathematics were composed by Kemetic scholars (Asante, 2019).

- The Rhind papyrus introduced the world to Kemetic mathematics and geometry.

- The development of mathematics and geometry in Kmt was due in part to the flooding of the Hapi.

  - Boundaries lines between farmers were washed away; thus it was necessary to develop a way to reestablish those boundaries.

MARTIN R. DELANY

BRIEF AUTHOR BIO

- Was accepted to Harvard Medical School & operated his own medical practice

- Partnered with Frederick Douglass to create *The North Star* newspaper

- Encouraged and believed Africans in the U.S. should return to Africa

- Began publishing his own newspaper, *The Mystery* - 1843

- Led emigration tours to West Africa in search of a new home for Africans leaving the U.S.

Sources: blackpast.org/african-american-history/delany-major-martin-robison-1812-1885/

THE ORIGIN OF RACES AND COLOR

MANUSCRIPT TYPE: Book

Main Points from the Text:

a. Construction of the pyramids indicated that Kemetic scholars had a knowledge of the science of conic sections and trigonometry.

b. The mdu nTr used by the Kemites was thought to have been taught to them by the Kushites of ancient Ethiopia (Delany, 1991).

- Greek writer and historian, Diodorus is cited as having seen both the Kushites and Kemites using their own form of mdu nTr; although he was convinced the ancient Kushites developed it first.

c. The literature of the Israelites, both science of letters and government, as well as religion were derived from Africans.

d. The Ethiopians were responsible for the invention of astronomy and astrology, thus teaching this to the Kemites (Delany, 1991).

DR. YOSEF BEN-JOCHANNAN

BRIEF AUTHOR BIO

- Was chairman of the African Studies Committee - UNESCO

- Donated his entire library of some 35,000 books to the Nation of Islam

- Led archaeological digs in the Nubia area of Egypt

- Led annual tours of Egypt for Africans

- Wrote several books, such as *Black Man of the Nile, African Origins of the Major "Western Religions,"* & *We the Black Jews*

Sources: blackpast.org/african-american-history/ben-jochannan-yosef-1918/

AFRICA: MOTHER OF WESTERN CIVILIZATION

MANUSCRIPT TYPE: Book

Main Points from the Text:

a. In addition to being taught in Kmt, the Greeks also received much of their education from the looting of libraries and sacking of Kemetic temples (ben-Jochannan, 1988).

b. The oft forgotten about library of Meneptheion, which was located in Waset (Thebes to the Greeks; Luxor to the Arabs), was one such library that was also ransacked and looted by the Greeks.

- This library was started by Seti I and was ultimately finished by Rameses II (ben-Jochannan, 1988).

- Virtually nothing has been written about the contents of the Meneptheion after it was looted during the Greek colonial period in Kmt.

c. Vast numbers of Greeks left their homelands for the opportunity to receive an education in Kmt (ben-Jochannan, 1988).

- These large migrations for the purpose of education shows that the Greeks were aware of how inadequately developed their schools and education system was in comparison with Kmt's.

d. Plato spent more than 12 years in exile, most of which he was studying under African teachers in the Mysteries System of Kmt (ben-Jochannan, 1988).

- The Athenian government resented the fact that Plato spent so much time in the company of African educators in Kmt learning a foreign philosophy.

e. 10,000 B.C.E. marks the date of the appearance of mankind's first known calendar (ben-Jochannan, 1988).

  - 4100 B.C.E. saw the appearance in Kmt of the earliest known solar calendar.

f. Kemetic scholars developed a theory of philosophy that was rooted in salvation and the deification of man.

  - Kemetic philosophers taught that if man's soul is freed from the body, it would enable him to become god-like.

  - The Greeks based their philosophy on the same fundamental Kemetic philosophical principles.

    • Plotinus, a Greek philosopher, stated:

"... The liberation of the mind from its finite consciousness is salvation" (ben-Jochannan, 1988, p. 375).

g. The following shows a chronological list of notable Pre-Socratic Greek philosophers who have links to ancient Kmt (ben-Jochannan, 1988, p. 389-390):

640 B.C.E. –Thales – completed all of his foundational education in Kmt. Anaximander and Anaximenes followed suit and also studied in Kmt.

576 B.C.E. – Xenophanes, Paramenides, Zeno, and Melissus also received an education in Kmt. They traveled to both Italy and Greece sharing the teachings they had learned from the African Mysteries System.

540 B.C.E. – Pythagoras completed his education in Kmt. He eventually made his way to

West Greece and began teaching what he had learned from Kemetic scholars in the Mysteries System.

530 B.C.E. – Heraclitus, Empedocles, Anaxgoras, and Democritus were educated in Kemetic schools in their native Samos.

460
or
457 B.C.E. – Herodotus journeyed to Kmt to receive an education from the African scholar priests. In Kmt, he studied in a number of different fields, such as history, science, philosophy, and religion.

h. Pliny and Herodotus, among others, proclaimed that Pythagoras was initiated into the Kemetic priesthood and received the secret knowledge of the priests, which undoubtedly included philosophy.

i. Studying to enter the priesthood in Kmt could be considered the equivalent of obtaining a doctorate degree (Ph.D.) today.

THE BLACK MAN'S NORTH & EAST AFRICA

MANUSCRIPT TYPE: Book

Main Points from the Text:

a. Many religious texts were developed by the Kemites. A few examples being the Pyramid and Coffin Texts.

    ▪ Some of these writings have been credited to biblical figures, such as Job and King Solomon.

b. Imhotep designed the Step Pyramid at Saqqara to rise in six sections that were not equal for a combined height of 204 ft (62 m).

    ▪ The base measurements were "411 ft (125 m) from east to west, and 358 ft (109 m) from north to south" (ben-Jochannan & Simmonds, 2005, p. 83).

- It would seem that little has been found concerning the reasoning behind why the Step Pyramid had the dimensions that it did. It is known, however, that during its construction, the building plans were changed a minimum of four times (Finch, 2007).

c. The oldest known form of family planning in the form of scientific birth control was developed and recorded by the Kemites in 1550 B.C.E (ben-Jochannan & Simmonds, 2005).

  - Information about this can be found in the Eber's Papyrus.

d. The system of a father teaching his occupation to his son was widely practiced in Kmt.

DR. NA'IM AKBAR

BRIEF AUTHOR BIO

- Chairman – Psychology Dept. – Morehouse College

- Fmr. President of the National Association of Black Psychologists (ABPsi)

- Authored as many as 8 books, such as *The Community of Self & Light From Ancient Africa*

- Received his Ph.D. in Clinical Psychology – University of Michigan

- Penned the essay *Mental Disorder Among African Americans* – outlining four main categories of mental illness among African Americans

KNOW THYSELF

MANUSCRIPT TYPE: Book

Main Points from the Text:

a. Multi-genius and scholar Imhotep developed medical techniques that influenced Greek scholars, such as Hippocrates (Akbar, 1999).

    ▪ Imhotep was worshipped in Greece as their god of medicine, and was referred to as Asclepius.

b. Kemetic scholars carefully studied various animals found in the Hapi Valley (Akbar, 1999).

    ▪ The scholars studied these animals in order to better understand the desirable traits the animals display. These virtuous traits became symbols that represented characteristics that people should make a part of our nature.

- By studying these animals, Kemetic scholars intended to reveal humanity's connection to nature and vice versa.

- Hor-em-akhet (Sphinx) is probably the most notable example of the connection between nature and one's self.

  - Hor-em-akhet possesses the body of a lion and the head of man. The lion's body is symbolic of fierceness and physical power seen in nature. The head of man was representative of humanity's control over their *animal nature* (Akbar, 1999, p. 47).

LIGHT FROM ANCIENT AFRICA

MANUSCRIPT TYPE: Book

Main Points from the Text:

a. In the Kemetic worldview, all things were connected. As such, attempting to distinguish between fields like physics, psychology, and so on had no purpose.

- This complete Afrikan worldview stood in direct opposition to the splintered European worldview and understanding of the universe (Akbar, 1994).

- The ancient Kemetic teachers made sure their students knew that, for example, one could not study geometry or medicine without studying the human being also; emphasizing the interconnectedness of all things.

b. The fields of numerology, alchemy, and astrology, for instance, were not pseudo sciences, as some European scholars alleged.

- Numerology, *"talks about the relationship between symbolic quantification and human expression"* (Akbar, 1994, p. 6).

- Alchemy, in ancient Kmt, focused on the relationship between the radical changing of materials in nature and the potential for dramatic change within the psyche of human beings.

- Ancient Kemetic astrology investigated the interconnection between the movements of humans and those of the stars and the heavens. Kemetic scientists discovered that human growth and advancement is linked to the progression of the stars.

    - European scholars, such as Professor of Psychology, Dr. John Ruscio (2006), have attacked astrology and alchemy (among other fields of study) as being pseudo science.

Ruscio wrote (2006):

> "Almost every science has... pseudosciences to deal with... astronomy has astrology; chemistry has alchemy" (p. 6).

c. The European worldview distorts the fact that ancient Kemetic scholars engaged in scientific research that was absolute and symbolic, experimental and hidden (Akbar, 1994).

d. Kemetic scholars wrote powerful accounts concerning their understanding that the human soul must live on. These accounts can be found in the tombs that have been discovered throughout Kmt.

e. The Kemites wrote about seven different dimensions of the human soul. The following is a compressed summary of those dimensions (Akbar, 1994, p. 9-12):

- First dimension: **Ka** – A person's physical body. The Ka is broken down into three parts: Divine Ka, Intermediate Ka, and Inferior Ka. The aim of a person was to evolve and grow their Ka from the Inferior stage to the highest level or Divine Ka stage.

- Second dimension: **Ba** – The essence of all things. It is this essence which is breathed into each individual. The ancient Kemetic scholars saw this essence as a breath entering one's being to give it life.

- Third dimension: **Khaba** – The celestial body; the equivalent would be the idea of a ghost. The Khaba oversees, in part, the processing of one's senses (hearing, vision, taste, smell, and touch), circulation of one's blood, and rhythm to name a few. Western society refers to as 'being possessed' is actually a person Khaba showing itself.

- Fourth dimension: **Akhu** – The Akhu is depicted as the center of knowledge and "mental perception" (p. 11). Kemetic scholars saw the Akhu as the place where the puzzle of the mind is to be solved and understood.

- Fifth dimension: **Seb** – The Seb is the spirit of 'adolescence' or 'puberty', and does not reveal itself until a person reaches those stages in their development. The Seb, in effect, is the reproductive power of humans.

- Sixth dimension: **Putah** – The Putah was indentified with coming of age mentally for a person; the joining together of one's brain and mind. This unification of the brain and mind creates the human identity.

- Seventh dimension: **Atum** – The Atum is known to be the "divine or eternal soul".

PART II:

THE

NON-AFRIKAN

WRITERS

THOMAS J. MCEVOY

BRIEF AUTHOR BIO

- Founder – McEvoy School of Pedagogy - NY

- Was editor of McEvoy Magazine

- Authored other titles, such as *Science of Education & Methods in Education*

Sources: The Epitome of History and Principles of Education

EPITOME OF HISTORY

&

PRINCIPLES OF EDUCATION

MANUSCRIPT TYPE: Book

Main Points from the Text:

a. The aim of priestly education was to uphold the superior position of the priests in Kemetic society.

b. Women in Kmt were given some type of education

   ▪ Women in Kmt also educated their children in the home (McEvoy, 1915).

c. Education was distributed according to one's "caste" position in Kmt (priest, warrior/soldier, or producer) but this "caste" system was not controlled by the State.

- It should be noted that the original concept of "caste," was unknown to the invading Aryan hordes. This point is addressed further in the section of the book titled *The People of Kemet* (McEvoy, 1915).

d. Elementary education began being available to students at five years of age.

- Subjects taught included: Reading, writing, arithmetic, geometry, and astronomy (McEvoy, 1915, p. 28).

- Religious training was given to all students, regardless of gender.

e. Young girls in Kmt were allowed to receive some education through private institutions and tutors.

f. The teaching methods of Kemetic teachers included: Having students imitate the teacher, recitation, memorization tasks, learning numbers through the playing of games, and using a stylus and wood, and ink on papyri (McEvoy, 1915).

g. Higher education for priests and soldiers consisted of: Engineering, language, natural Science, astronomy, mathematics, medicine, philosophy, religion, and music (McEvoy, 1915, p. 28).

h. Colleges in Kmt were in the temples. The "top" or prestigious colleges were located at: Ineb-hedj/Men-nefer (Memphis), Waset (Thebes/Luxor), On (Heliopolis)

DR. NIKOLAOS LAZARIDIS

BRIEF AUTHOR BIO

- Received his Master's degree & Ph.D. from Oxford University

- Asst. Prof. –Ancient Mediterranean History – California State University

Sources: linkedin.com/in/nikolaos-lazaridis-67937b7b

EDUCATION

&

APPRENTICESHIP

MANUSCRIPT TYPE: Research Article

Main Points from the Text:

a. Education is a special institution or system, not a general idea comprised of various forms of teaching and learning (Lazaridis, 2010).

- In line with Eurocentric analyses of Kmt, education in Africa; Kmt especially, is almost always described as not having been a specialized institution or system.

b. Based on the presupposition that there is a difference in the relationship between home and school learning at the core of Kemetic education, the study of ancient Kemetic education excludes children learning at home (the home is not a special institution).

c. Home education/home schooling was just as important a pedagogical method as standardized schooling (Lazaridis, 2010).

d. It is likely that the majority of workers in Kmt received an education in a "domestic" environment, instead of in a "school" environment (Lazaridis, 2010).

  - The artisan village of Pa-demi or Set Maa (Deir el-Medina to the Arabs) located in the Kemetic city of Waset, provides evidence of the home training mentioned above.

e. Different from today, the Kemetic education system offered only basic and not advanced training overall.

f. The narrowness of the Kemetic education system resulted in outlined curriculum content (Lazaridis, 2010).

g. There are a number of surviving copies of school exercises done primarily on pottery, stone ostraca (potshards with writing/drawings etched into it), wooden and stone tablets, and small papyrus fragments (Lazaridis, 2010).

- These copies cover a range of periods in Kemetic history. Bresciani et al. (1983); Kaplony-Heckel (1974); Vernus (1984) confirm the existence of the above mentioned schoolwork exercises.

h. It is not yet clear, the exact differences between Kemetic .texts produced by seshu (scribes) and the copies produced by students.

i. The word in the Kemetic language in reference to a school as an institute was *per-aa*, meaning "House of Life."

- Scholars are still debating the meaning of *per-aa*, with some scholars divided between *"House of Life"* and *"scriptorium"* (which is where the seshu worked) as possible meanings (Lazaridis, 2010).

j. The average age of Kemites who entered school was approximately four to five years.

k. Children in Kmt learned geography, geometry, reading, writing, basic mathematics (Lazaridis, 2010).

l. With the arrival of the New Kingdom dynasties, there is evidence that children in Kmt were learning foreign languages in schools.

  - The teaching of foreign languages in schools corresponded historically with the period of Kemetic imperialism and foreign relations (Brunner, 1991; Fischer-Elfert, 2001).

m. Limited evidence exists that suggests music, sports, and other activities of the arts were taught in addition to the basic or core curriculum (Lazaridis, 2010).

n. Students in Kmt studied literature from earlier time periods in Kemetic history. Evidence of this comes from the New Kingdom period where students studied older texts from the Middle Kingdom period.

o. Students in Kmt practiced spelling and grammar by continually copying passages delivered orally by their teachers.

- The children also copied parts of authentic or "pseudo" documents, which were referred to as "miscellanies" (the authorship of these 'miscellanies' is unknown) that were possibly compilations created by teachers for classroom use (Lazaridis, 2010).

p. Students in Kmt were also learning how to read and write by using material found on the insides of various tombs.

- This is due to tombs being also meant for preserving literary works.

q. Changes in the educational developments of Kmt most likely followed the developments in language (Lazaridis, 2010).

r. Students in Kmt were more than likely taught the Hieratic writing style, which was replaced later by the Demotic writing style.

- This change took place during the Hellenistic period when Greek became the official language in Alexandria.

  - Being that this was the case, officials added Greek to curricula in Kmt.

s. Beginning in the second century C.E., the Coptic writing style eventually took the place of Demotic writing in schools.

DR. ERNEST C. RICHARDSON

BRIEF AUTHOR BIO

- Theologian, Librarian, & Scholar

- Received an Honorary Ph.D. – Washington & Jefferson College

- Was librarian for Princeton University

- Was President of the American Library Association

Sources: en.wikipedia.org/wiki/Ernest_Cushing_Richardson

SOME OLD EGYPTIAN LIBRARIANS

MANUSCRIPT TYPE: Book

Main Points from the Text:

a. Kemetic universities were inside of libraries that were managed by the librarians.

b. The grandson of Per-Aa Khufu (King of the Fourth Dynasty and responsible for the building of the Great Pyramid) went to school and became a writer in the *House of Books* (Richardson, 1911).

c. Per-Aa Akhenaton had a palace library (ca. 1370 B.C.E.), and so did Per-Aa Nefirikare of the Fifth Dynasty (ca. 2470 B.C.E.) (Richardson, 1911).

d. Djhuti/Tehuti was the most supreme of the Kemetic librarians. Seshait, wife of Djhuti/Tehuti, was the "Lady of Libraries"

- Seshait is also the patron of architects and librarians and was considered the goddess of history.

e. Commoners were kept away from books, as it was believed that books gave supernatural powers to those who read them (Richardson, 1911).

- A story is mentioned of a librarian who was sentenced to death for having borrowed one of Per-Aa Ramses III's books of magic to someone they should not have.

f. The earliest form of systematic history known in literature is the book of annals of Kemetic per-Aas that are on the Palermo Stone (Richardson, 1911).

g. The Kemites felt that all forms of expression, particularly, written expression, indicated intelligence.

- The Kemites saw books as a cure for ignorance, as there was a symbolic relationship between written words and immortality in Kmt.

MORRIS KLINE

BRIEF AUTHOR BIO

- Felt that math was crucial to humans understanding their environments

- Long time critic of how math was being taught

- Received his Bachelor's, Master's & Ph.D. from New York University

- Was a professor at New York University

- Authored numerous books, like *Mathematics and the Search for Knowledge* & *Mathematics in Western Culture*

Sources: nytimes.com/1992/06/11/nyregion/morris-kline-84-math-professor-and-critic-of-math-teaching-dies.html

MATHEMATICAL THOUGHT FROM ANCIENT TO MODERN TIMES

MANUSCRIPT TYPE: Book

Main Points from the Text:

a. Main surviving papyri for mathematics are the Moscow papyrus that is in Moscow, and the Rhind papyrus, which is being housed in the British Museum. Both papyri are dated at around 1700 B.C.E. (Kline, 1972).

- The seshu (scribe) Ahmes (ca. 1650 B.C.E.) wrote the Ahmes (so-called Rhind) Papyrus. Although there is some disagreement about whether or not Ahmes himself wrote the papyrus or copied and annotated it (see Encyclopaedia Britannica, 2020; Heilbron, 2020).

b. Math was reportedly known to the Kemites as early as 3500 B.C.E., possibly before then but very little development occurred from then until Kmt was conquered by Greece (Kline, 1972).

c. The Moscow and Ahmes (Rhind) papyri contain equations that are comparable to linear equations of today.

   ▪ Some scholars are of the belief that the seshu Ahmes wrote the Ahmes (Rhind) papyrus in the form of a textbook for those who were studying math at that time (Kline, 1972).

d. With Kemetic mathematics, there was no separation of geometry from the rest of mathematics (Kline, 1972).

e. Herodotus claimed that mathematics in Kmt came about because of the yearly inundation or flooding of the Hapi (Nile) river.

- Every year boundary lines for land belonging to farmers needed to be re-established.

f. Math problems were often done verbally in Kemetic schools.

g. The Kemites used math to determine total wages to be paid to laborers, find the volumes of granaries, and collect taxes (Kline, 1972)

- Another use of mathematics in Kmt was in the construction of buildings and calculating how many blocks were necessary to build them.

h. A combination of astronomy and geometry were used to build Kemetic temples in distinct ways to allow sunlight to hit them at certain angles (Kline, 1972).

i. Mathematics in astronomy made the creation of the calendar possible, which was completed before Kmt became a nation.

DR. FRANK P. GRAVES

Brief Author Bio

- Received two Ph.D.s from Columbia University

- Taught at Columbia University & Tufts College

- Was President of University of Washington

- Was Commissioner of Education – New York

Sources: en.wikipedia.org/wiki/Frank_Pierrepont_Graves

A HISTORY OF EDUCATION BEFORE THE MIDDLE AGES

MANUSCRIPT TYPE: Book

Main Points from the Text:

a. Due to the annual flooding of the Hapi (Nile), the Kemites were forced to quickly develop and perfect engineering techniques (Graves, 1909).

b. Women in Kmt did have access to education but nothing beyond the very basics.

c. The knowledge obtained by the Kemites to erect pyramids, etc., was obtained through empirical research (Graves, 1909).

d. The mathematics used by the Kemites to build the pyramids was not an actual science.

- Kemetic mathematical methods were criticized for appearing clumsy and awkward, in part due to the apparent sparse usage of fractions.

e. Education in Kmt was held in very high esteem only because of the practical use of it.

   - The Kemites were pragmatists when it came to learning.

f. Students were taught subjects and acquired the skills that were needed in Kmt.

g. The Kemites focused more on the acquisition of professional skills in education (Graves, 1909).

h. The average length of a school day for children in Kmt was approximately half the day.

i. The average age for admission into school for children was exactly five years old.

j. The government did not ensure that any educational system was available for the general population of Kmt.

k. Teachers were supposedly in great abundance, and at a fairly cheap rate.

l. The foremost colleges in Kmt could be found at the temples of: Ptah at Ineb-hedj, Re at Ann, and Amon at Waset.

m. There was a high rate of illiteracy in Kmt. Due to the illiteracy rates, seshu were on the whole not needed (Graves, 1909).

n. Those who were educated as architects, aside from learning mathematics and mechanics, also learned history.

o. Students who studied to become physicians learned crude anatomy and physiology.

   ▪ They received specific training with regards to vital organs.

p. Learning to write in Kmt seemed to have been done in graduated steps (Graves, 1909).

- School children would first write upon wooden tablets with a stylus, and then they would begin transcribing from dictation on papyrus.

- There has been no type of grammar or vocabulary book found, which indicated that students learned most writing by imitation.

- Copybooks from children practicing their writing were found in trash heaps in Kmt, easily identified by the corrections made by the teachers.

q. A strict code of discipline was maintained in Kemetic schools. Maxims were often used by Kemetic teachers in disciplining their students (Graves, 1909). One such example is:

> 'A boy's ears are on his back; he hears when he is beaten.'

- Confinement to the temple where a student may have been learning was reportedly used as a form of punishment.

ADOLF ERMAN

BRIEF AUTHOR BIO

- Egyptologist & Lexicographer

- Was Assoc. & Full Prof. – University of Berlin

- Was Dir. of Egyptian Dept. – Royal Museum - Germany

- Researched Egyptian grammar extensively

- Authored more than 10 books, including *Egyptian Grammar: With Tables of Signs, Bibliography, Exercises for Reading and Glossary*

Sources: *en.wikipedia.org/wiki/Adolf_Erman*

LIFE IN ANCIENT EGYPT

MANUSCRIPT TYPE: Book

Main Points from the Text:

a. The Kemites valued learning for the superiority and power and control it gave to the educated over those considered to be uneducated (Erman, 1894).

b. Those who followed the learning professions, for example, a scribe, were exempt from manual labor.

c. Many students would pray to Djhuti/Tehuti, who is the god of writing and learning.

d. Young boys in Kmt, who intended on becoming seshu (scribes), no matter of their rank, were sent to the *instruction house*, which was a school (Erman, 1894).

  ▪ They studied in the same classes with children of princes, also meant to become seshu.

e. Various government departments of the New Kingdom in Kmt had their own specialized schools.

- At those schools, candidates for those departments received their education and training.

f. Seshu and teachers of high positions were assigned a number of pupils that they were responsible for teaching/tutoring.

g. Pupils wrote to their tutors:

   "I was with thee since I was brought up as a child; thou didst beat my back and thy instructions went into my ear" (Erman, 1894, p. 329).

h. It was possible for a young man in Kmt to pursue a career in a different field of study from the one that he was originally educated in at school.

- The High Priest of Amon, Bekenchons, is one such example of someone who switched fields of study (Erman, 1894).

- Bekenchons also stated that from age five to sixteen, he was *captain in the royal stable for education*, and had entered the temple of Amon priesthood at the lowest rank.

i. Teachers in Kmt justified their disciplinary methods by likening them to breaking-in wild animals to breaking-in young seshu (Erman, 1894).

  - Strongly cautioning students was also effective in disciplining students.

j. Teachers would give their students *shayts* or instructions to copy. Usually, the material that was relevant to what they were studying.

k. It was felt to be very important for young scholars to have his copybook with him in his tomb at the time of his death rather than his favorite book to read.

  - Young scholars in Kmt understood the value of good writing.

l. Books that Kemetic schoolchildren copied their lessons in were identified by: Size and shape, short pages containing a few long lines, and teacher's corrections on the upper edge(s) of the pages (Erman, 1894).

m. Evidence has been reported of a student's copybook from Kmt with the dates twenty-third, twenty-fourth, and twenty-fifth of Epiphi, the eleventh month of the Kemetic calendar, written on the right-hand side of the pages, signifying a daily writing task.

n. The Kemites considered writing to be the building block of all education (Erman, 1894).

THE LITERATURE
OF THE ANCIENT EGYPTIANS

MANUSCRIPT TYPE: Book

Main Points from the Text:

a. In the New Kingdom period (ca. 1554 B.C.E.), the Kemites had a system of education that developed their knowledge, thus allowing it to be passed down (Erman, 1927).

b. The Kemetic system of education is broken down into two stages; a lower and an upper.

    ▪ The lower stage would be similar to what we today would call school (Erman, 1927, p 185).

c. At school, the young boys were taught ancient literature and writing.

- This writing practice was done using thin pieces of limestone and potsherds (fragments of pottery).

- Papyrus rolls were much too expensive to be used for writing practice (Erman, 1927).

d. There was a school that was attached to the temple; the Ramesseum as it is popularly called.

- Ramses II (Ramses the Great) built it in tribute to the manifestation of the Creator, Amun on the west bank of Waset.

- Young Kemetic boys who studied at this temple used three particular texts often (Erman, 1927):

    - Instruction(s) of King Amenemhet.

    - Instruction(s) of Duauf.

    - Hymn to the Hapi (Nile).

e. The Sallier and the Anastasi papyri originated in Ineb-hedj/Men-nefer (Memphis).

- In addition, the three texts that formed the Sallier and the Anastasi papyri were the core subjects of the curriculum taught in Kemetic schools.

f. After young Kemetic boys finished elementary schooling, they began to study as seshu (scribes) in a type of administration under an elder official who was usually to be their superior (Erman, 1927).

- It was at the level of higher education that students were copying as many as three pages per day, instead of the few lines characteristic of the elementary level.

g. Simple tasks, such as writing a single word in hieroglyphs were taken very seriously and done with great care.

h. When it comes to the warnings given to school boys in Kmt, there are pieces of writing that discuss the condition of being a scribe compared to other jobs in the so-called Papyrus Anastasi.

i. There are countless compositions to and from seshu, about how to treat a wife and a mother, and even love songs.

MIRIAM LICHTHEIM

BRIEF AUTHOR BIO

- Was a translator of ancient Egyptian writings

- Received her Ph.D. in Egyptology – University of Chicago

- Was Academic Librarian at Yale University & UCLA

Sources: en.wikipedia.org/wiki/Miriam_Lichtheim

ANCIENT EGYPTIAN LITERATURE VOL. II

MANUSCRIPT TYPE: Book

Main Points from the Text:

a. Many of the short prayers found in various papyri of the Ramesside Age, due to their general character, were used as example exercises for students to copy in school.

b. The punctuation marks used by Ramesside seshu (scribes) were usually black or red dots (Lichtheim, 2006).

  ▪ The punctuation marks occur both in verse-point and prose texts.

c. A number of texts from the Ramesside period discuss an education system in Kmt that trained young men to become seshu or civil servants (Lichtheim, 2006).

- Not all instruction happened within a school.

  - Documents show that students were taught in a more personal capacity, with a senior official guiding and teaching the student.

d. All works of literature, letters, and documents dealing with legal and business matters came to be utilized as school texts.

e. The Lansing papyrus is a school text in the sense that it was focused on the theme of being a scribe (Lichtheim, 2006).

- This text looks at the teacher-student relationship in a series of eleven parts.

f. Kemetic students learned how to write by copying down a variety of popular and important writing from even earlier times (Lichtheim, 2006).

- It was believed that by copying the writings, the students would gain the necessary penmanship and reading comprehension skills.

- In addition to acquiring the literacy skills, Kemetic teachers hoped by having the students copy down the texts that the students' minds would be shaped by what they saw in the texts.

E. L. KEMP

- Was Prof. of Pedagogy – Keystone State Normal School - PA

- Was also Prof. of Ancient Languages – Keystone State Normal School - PA

- Also author of *An Idyl of the War: The German Exiles, and Other Poems*

Sources:

The History of Education

An Idyl of the War: The German Exiles, and Other Poems

HISTORY OF EDUCATION

MANUSCRIPT TYPE: Book

Main Points from the Text:

a. Many of the younger nations, who came after Kmt, received their first lessons in what a civilization is, what a they look like, how a civilization operates, etc., right on the banks of the Hapi (Nile) (Kemp, 1902).

b. The impression that Kemetic intelligence had on the Greeks was quite clear when studying the significant religious beliefs of Greek education and art.

c. The art works of the Kemites showed skill and a degree of creativeness, and they showcased their intelligence and taste through their artwork.

d. Seshu (scribes) had almost exclusive control over higher education in Kmt (Kemp, 1902).

e. There was no state provision for educating the general population in Kmt.

f. There were enough private teachers and schools in the various communities in Kmt to be able to educate the young children of tradespeople and artisans (Kemp, 1902).

   - These private schools taught basic level reading, writing, and arithmetic.

g. The occupation of seshu (scribe) attracted mostly middle class people who were eager and motivated enough to pursue the role.

h. There was a great need for seshu due to a need for copying sacred manuscripts, and preparing official documents and records (Kemp, 1902).

i. After finishing elementary school, young boys began training under seshu in various offices.

   - One of their first training duties was to copy and commit to memory legal procedures, documents, etc.

j. What some Egyptologists are considering as higher education, seshu received at temple schools (Kemp, 1902).

- It was at the temple schools that they were taught: Arithmetic, Administration, Law; Demotic, Hieratic, and mdu nTr (hieroglyphic) writing styles.

k. There was indeed a mysteries system of knowledge in Kmt, as the following passage indicates:

"It is probable that some of their religious conceptions were of a high order, but the highest of them, as well as other portions of their learning, were treated as mysteries and reserved for the priests of superior rank" (Kemp, 1902, p. 43).

l. The main college locations of the priests were located at: Ineb-hedj/Men-nefer, Waset, Ann.

m. The "cultured class" studied and read extensive amounts of literature, which mostly consisted of:

technical treatises, letters, books of travel, novels, poems, and moral and religious texts (Kemp, 1902).

n. Many of the pieces of Kemetic literature: poems, stories, and so on, are "good" but do not contain much literary worth.

o. The education of the general population in Kmt was not the type of education that elevated or helped one's life to progress forward.

p. Much of the medical knowledge that the Kemites possessed was primitive and involved an awkward blending of magic and exorcisms.

- There were, however, some specialists in Kmt, such as those physicians who were responsible for the embalming process.

DR. HENDRIK W. VAN LOON

BRIEF AUTHOR BIO

- Received his Ph.D. – University of Munich

- Historian, Journalist, & Children's Author

- Was Prof. of History – Antioch College - OH

- Authored numerous titles, including his most famous *The Story of Mankind*

- Was a correspondent for the Assoc. Press during the Russian Revolution - 1905

Sources: en.wikipedia.org/wiki/Hendrik_Willem_van_Loon

ANCIENT MAN: THE BEGINNING OF CIVILIZATIONS

MANUSCRIPT TYPE: Book

Main Points from the Text:

a. In the chapter titled *Earliest* School, Van Loon (1922) recognized the antiquity of the Kemites by saying:

> *"The oldest center of civilization developed in the valley of the Nile, in a country which was called Egypt"* (p. 35).

b. Many of the modern conveniences and technologies we possess today are a result of the accomplishments of the Kemites, among other groups (also Babylonians and Phoenicians).

c. The credit for the development of language, as well as writing goes to the Kemites.

- Speaking of forming a writing system and who was responsible for it is best summed up by the following passage:

  "It took the human race hundreds of thousands of years to discover this and the credit for it goes to the Egyptians" (Van Loon, 1922, p. 40).

- Van Loon (1922) proclaimed that the mdu nTr developed by the ancient Kemites is much better looking than our current alphabet but much more complex.

d. When the Romans entered Kmt as conquerors and upon seeing the vast libraries and learning centers, showed little to no regard for or interest in them (Van Loon, 1922).

e. The Arab and Turkish conquerors that later conquered Kmt showed the same abhorrence and ignorance, and disgust that the Romans did toward all Kemetic literature and writing that was not in line with what the Qur'an taught.

f. There were Europeans who visited Kmt after the Arabs conquered it, to study the sculptures, architecture, literature, and so on.

- The Europeans were as knowledgeable about these topics as the Romans and Turks before them (which were not very knowledgeable at all); as there was no one present to provide explanations (Van Loon, 1922).

DR. ROSS G. MURISON

BRIEF AUTHOR BIO

- Also authored *Babylonia and Assyria, A Sketch of their History & The Mythical Serpents of Hebrew Literature*

- Was a lecturer & scholar of Oriental Languages – University College - Toronto

---

Sources: Murison's History of Egypt

HISTORY OF EGYPT

MANUSCRIPT TYPE: Book

Main Points from the Text:

a. Work in Kmt was very well organized, with each occupation having and choosing its own elected spokesperson (Murison, 1951).

   ■ Evidence of this is in the form of a tablet that lies in the British Museum that lists those elected foremen for each group, their workers and the workers' attendance.

b. Kemetic literature was explained as having little actual literary value. The *Book of Coming Forth by Day and by Night* was described as containing some passages that were exceptional (Murison, 1951).

   ■ Hymns that were written in dedication to Ra were considered beautiful but "most of the hymns are full of stereotyped phrases suitable for any king or god, and contain nothing devotional" (Murison, 1951, p. 98).

c. Schoolmasters placed a high level of importance on writing one's letter in the correct way. There are several examples of their models that still survive.

d. One of the signs of "culture" in the Kemetic education process was the use of a lot of foreign vocabulary.

e. The Kemites were possibly trained to use "kiln-dried bricks" to build homes for the upper class as they were a more expensive building material (Murison, 1951).

f. Whenever the Hapi (Nile) flooded, precise measurements had to be taken so that each farmer reclaimed the correct amount of land (Murison, 1951).

g. The area of a circle was figured out by the Kemites and not of the triangle, and the way that the Kemites discovered the area of a circle was sloppy.

h. Credit for the invention of astronomy and its introduction into Kmt goes to the Babylonians (Murison, 1951).

- After the introduction of astronomy from Babylonia, the Kemites made substantial progress in the field of astronomy:

- The Kemites charted thirty-six constellations, having documented the names and positions of those stars.

- At least five of the planets had been known to the Kemites for a considerable amount of time, and were carefully studied by them.

  - Kemetic astronomers were able to describe the colors of the five planets known to them among other aspects of the planets' appearance.

- The important temples throughout Kmt doubled as observatories.

i. Djhuti/Tehuti and the moon taught the Kemites the act of measuring time in months.

  - Each month was named after the manifestation of the Creator that cares for it (Murison, 1952).

j. The Kemites aimed for high levels of perfection when it came to the mechanical arts and building things.

  - One such example was a statue of Pepi discovered that was constructed by skilled workers made entirely of copper.

DR. SAMUEL G. WILLIAMS

BRIEF AUTHOR BIO

- Also authored *A History of Medieval Education* & *A History of Modern Education*

- Was a professor at Cornell University

Sources: AHistory of Ancient Education

THE HISTORY OF ANCIENT EDUCATION

MANUSCRIPT TYPE: Book

Main Points from the Text:

a. At the fifth year, parents in Kmt began to incorporate education into their children's daily lives. This included the priestly teaching of the essential elements of: all learning, reading, writing, and reckoning (calculating) (Williams, 1903).

   ▪ It is unclear just how general or specific elementary education was in Kmt.

b. By 664 B.C.E., the writing system being used for reading and writing in elementary schools was the Demotic form (Williams, 1903).

- Demotic was supposedly more difficult to decode than the other writing forms, such as Hieratic.

c. In the advanced temple schools, Hieratic instead of Demotic was the writing system used (Williams, 1903).

d. The first known writing lessons were done with a reed stylus (Williams, 1903).

- Once the student(s) acquired adequate writing skills, they then began to write on papyrus with reed pens; using red and black inks.

e. When learning mathematics, students in Kmt counted on their fingers, with pebbles, and used the abacus (a tool used to make calculations) to help them.

- The Kemites and the Chinese are both given credit for developing an abacus.

f. Outside of the general education, priests were responsible for the education in the temples.

- Education was, by all accounts, accessible to children of all classes in Kmt.

- Even though schooling in the temples was available to all in Kmt, it was most likely the children of rich families that were able to take advantage, as education was very expensive.

g. Pursuing an education in Kmt allowed for careers in the high offices of the state (Williams, 1903).

h. Some of Kmt's early writings reveal just how much the Kemites valued education and impressed that upon the children.

i. The threat of being doomed to manual labor was used to convince children to choose education.

- Williams lists volume eight of the *Records of the Past* as evidence.

j. Much of the recovered Kemetic literature was saved in the copying or writing exercises of Kemetic students (Williams, 1903).

k. Ptahhotep's book is considered the oldest text on teaching methods in existence.

l. The Kemites showed a deep understanding of chemistry (Williams, 1903). Some examples of this understanding included preparing colors, making glass and porcelain, and the embalming of those who have died.

m. The Kemites had an extensive knowledge of astronomy.

 - It was from the Kemites that the Greeks probably first derived their exposure to the study of astronomy, as well as geometry.

n. As a result of studying astronomy, the Kemites also began studying astrology; believing that celestial bodies had an effect on the lives of people (Williams, 1903).

o. The Kemites had developed a vast knowledge of geography as far back as the time of Moses.

- The geography and astronomy treatises that Ptolemy wrote in the second century C.E. was derived from both Kemetic and Greek sources (Williams, 1903).

p. As far back as 2,000 years B.C.E., there were collections of papyri in the libraries of Kmt that were so important that they required high officials to care for them (Williams, 1903).

- Williams mentioned the library at Alexandria and the 700,000 books it contained. He went further to proclaim that it would have been extremely difficult to collect such a number of books without printing and making and collecting books having existed in Kmt long before the arrival of the Greeks.

q. Plato praised the Kemetic approach to using objectivity when teaching school subjects.

HENRY IMMANUEL SMITH

BRIEF AUTHOR BIO

- Was Prof. of German and Literature – Theological Seminary – Gettysburg, PA

- Also was Prof. of Modern Languages – Pennsylvania College

Sources: The History of Education: Ancient and Modern

THE HISTORY OF EDUCATION: ANCIENT AND MODERN

MANUSCRIPT TYPE: Book

Main Points from the Text:

a. The caste system in Kmt was strictly enforced and the various jobs and education types were set according to respective castes (Smith, 1842).

b. Even though education in Kmt was separated by caste, it was highly effective and well managed.

c. It was at the learning institutions that the Kemites surpassed all contemporary nations of antiquity in the arts and sciences: astronomy, mathematics, geometry, arithmetic, chemistry, architecture, sculpting, painting, music, and medicine (Smith, 1842).

d. Kemetic scholars disseminated some of their knowledge to the public without revealing too many of their secrets.

e. The general population could read, write, and construct coded messages (Smith, 1842).

- Without the ability to write coded letters, women in Kmt would not have been able to conduct their business at the market.

- Children are also assumed to have been taught many of these branches of learning, so Kmt could not have been without common schools.

- Plato claimed that the children of Kmt learned reading together (Smith, 1842).

f. Fathers were responsible for teaching their sons mechanical trade skills. The same was true of children in the military caste.

- The sons and daughters of priests were better educated than children of other castes.

- Sons of the per-Aa received the very best of education.

- The classmates of the per-Aa's son(s) were the best educated of the priests' sons who were at least twenty years of age, contradicting some sources.

- The friends of the per-Aa's son(s) were selected based on how "cultured" they were (Smith, 1842).

  - This method was supposedly also used by the various monarchs of Asia.

g. The wives of the priests were far better educated than the wives belonging to others castes (Smith, 1842).

  - The priests' wives also had more time available to them to focus on the early education of their children.

h. Most other nations of antiquity had in some way degraded the position and importance of the role of women in their societies. This lessening of the woman's role had profoundly negative effects on the children in those societies, and eroded the quality of the education they received.

- When it comes to the education of the ancient Kemites, one can see the various positive aspects specific to their system of education. For example, maintaining a peaceful societal life during prosperous periods. One can also see the negative aspects of Kemetic education manifesting itself in the form of restricting intellectual growth and free thought.

W. M. FLINDERS PETRIE

Brief Author Bio

- Archaeologist & Egyptologist

- Was knighted in 1923

- Was Edwards Prof. of Egyptology – University College - London

- Most famous writings include Methods and Aims in Archaeology

- Performed excavations in Egypt until the age of 85

- "Discovered" the Merneptah stele

Sources:
britannica.com/biography/Flinders-Petrie
en.wikipedia.org/wiki/Flinders_Petrie

SOCIAL LIFE IN ANCIENT EGYPT

MANUSCRIPT TYPE: Book

Main Points from the Text:

a. Children in Kmt began their schooling at a very early age.

- Kemetic education could not have been effective as it did not lead to more advanced subjects (Petrie, 1923).

- The Kemetic education system was most likely a ritual of memorizing without truly understanding the meaning.

b. Potsherds were used in the beginning stages of writing development in Kmt (Petrie, 1923).

c. Mistake filled writing can be found in all ages of those who were learning writing in Kmt.

d. Education in Kmt, after the invasion and occupation of the Persians remained high in quality.

e. Education in the city of Alexandria suffered after the killings and exiles under Ptolemy Physcon, ca: 140 B.C.E. (Petrie, 1923).

- The school of learning in the Museum was splintered, with instructors fleeing to various islands and Greek cities to restart educational institutions.

PIERRE MONTET

Brief Author Bio

- Egyptologist – conducted excavations in the Nile Delta

- Notable writing include *Eternal Egypt* & *Everyday Life in the Days of Ramses the Great*

- Led significant excavation –Byblos (Jubayl, Lebanon)

- Was Prof. of Egyptology – University of Strasbourg & Collège de France – Paris

---

Sources: britannica.com/biography/Pierre-Montet

ETERNAL EGYPT

MANUSCRIPT TYPE: Book

Main Points from the Text:

a. The Kemites had a plethora of vocabulary for all things linked to daily routines and tasks (Montet, 1964).

- The people of Kmt found ways to develop and put abstract thought into practice.

b. Up until the conquest of Kmt by the Romans, the Kemites continued to develop and introduce new characters in mdu nTr (Montet, 1964).

- During this time, the Kemites continued to try making the mdu nTr more difficult to read.

- The seshu (scribes) enjoyed creating documents that required the reader to decipher the text, and even during the Greek and Roman occupations of Kmt, again the seshu took pride in creating texts that their colonizers could not understand.

c. The Kemites were pleased with having developed a writing system with so much power.

- This belief was so strong that the seshu (scribes) believed that in the case of the funerary texts, they had to remove or damages the mdu nTr that represented soldiers, animals in the wild, and so on. This act of defacing the mdu nTr was done to prevent any harm from coming to those who have passed on.

d. The evolution from mdu nTr to the Hieratic writing style should have led to a further evolution to an alphabet afterward.

e. Seshu were employed in prisons in Kmt.

f. Zedefra, Imhotep, and Ptahhotep were considered to be the first known professional writers ever written about in human history (Montet, 1964).

g. Copies of Kemetic literature were used to teach students writing. Some examples are (Montet, 1964):

- Tale of the Shipwrecked Sailor

- Dialogue of a Man Weary of Life with His Soul

- Tale of Two Brothers

- Maxims of Ani

- Children were copying texts onto limestone, rather than parchment or papyrus because the latter was unaffordable.

h. Collections of teachings were the earliest known literary category of Kemetic literature.

i. During the Pyramid Age, it was fashionable to express rules on good behavior in the form of maxims, which allowed for easy memorization.

j. The Kemites did create a genre of writing – pictures with a caption.

- Examples are provided on page 207.

k. A scholar named Kheti is credited with having written about the poor and the awful living conditions of the manual laborers in Kmt in his work *The Satire on Occupations* (Montet, 1964).

- Soldiers and priests were not included in the text but the advantages of being a royal scribe were glorified a great deal.

l. Prior to the Kemetic title *The Satire on Occupations* being written, another Kemetic title called *Kemit* was written that praises the profession of scribe also.

- It is thought that this book praised the position of priest because at one point, there was a severe lack of government workers due to civil wars being fought during the First Intermediate Period (ca. 2280 B.C.E.).

m. The Twelfth Dynasty (ca. 2052 B.C.E.) is a popular time in Kemetic history due in large part to the literary achievement of Kemetic writers.

- Montet (1964) remarked that:

  "...and it is to this same period," [speaking of the 12th dynasty] *"that we owe several imaginative works which are among the best Egypt ever produced"* (p. 212).

- Examples of the works mentioned above are:

  - *The Story of the Eloquent Peasant* (or *Oasis-Dweller*).

  - *The Story of Sinuhe*

n. Literature of the New Kingdom period (ca. 1554 B.C.E.) focused on hymns to the various manifestations or forms of the Creator: Amen/Amun, Amun-Ra/Amen-Ra, Re/Ra, Aton/Aten, etc.

o. Before and after the Armanian period, love songs emerged as a genre in Kemetic literature. Some examples are (Montet, 1964):

  - The Harris Papyrus 500

  - Chester Beatty Papyrus

- Turin Papyrus

- The theme present in the poems above focused on the idea of a woman's beauty (Montet. 1964).

  - The poets defined a woman's beauty in the same manner as they defined the beauty of the manifestations of the Creator.

- The Kemites considered gold, lapis lazuli, the lotus flower, and the Sirius star the most beautiful, which shows in their writing.

p. The heroic form of poetry was born out of the battles fought by Kemetic warriors in their war of liberation, conquest of Syria, and the battles against hostile foreign nations (Montet, 1964).

q. The use of a direct method of storytelling was used from the reign of Ramses II until around the Late Kingdom period (ca. 760 B.C.E.).

- Of the works produced using this style, Montet asserted:

"*The monotony of style and a certain lack of inventiveness which characterizes most of these works, are occasionally redeemed by some amusing episode...*" (Montet, 1964, p. 219).

r. The Moral Treatise of Amenemopet/Amenemope was the original design for the Proverbs of Solomon that was written at a much later time (ca. 700 B.C.E.) (Encyclopaedia Britannica, 2020).

s. Kmt never produced any writers that could stand in comparison to Greek writers, such as Homer, Pindar, Sophocles, or Herodotus.

t. As for the exact sciences that were being developed in Kmt:

"*In the opinion of the Greeks, the Ancient Egyptians were well versed in mathematics, astronomy and medicine...*" (Montet, 1964, p. 220).

u. Land surveyors measured royal land plots and private estates.

- The land surveyors also completed tax assessments.

v. Seshu were in charge of food supplies and to split up the various goods amongst the thousands of Kemites who were not given equal rights (Montet, 1964).

w. The system of counting used in Kmt was the decimal system (Montet, 1964).

- Numerical units were marked by strokes.

- Tens, hundreds, and thousands were indicated by phonetic signs.

x. There is artwork located at Beni-Hasan that shows an arithmetic lesson being acted out.

- There are two distinct steps in the painting: counting using one's fingers and performing arithmetic in one's head (Montet, 1964).

y. The Kemites were skilled in both, adding and subtracting.

- The Great Harris Papyrus provides examples of the Kemites adding together various items.

z. While there was an apparent absence of multiplication tables found, the method used by the Kemites of picture-writing simplified multiplying or dividing by ten.

aa. The way that knowledge and information was systematically organized in Kmt was absolutely scientific in nature.

- The Kemites also developed a system of arranging their mathematical knowledge.

bb. The calendar (which we use today) to serve agricultural purposes in Kmt.

- The inundation of the Hapi (Nile) lasted for approximately one-third of the year; the rest of the year was, "two more or less equal periods" (Montet, 1964, p.223).

- These divisions of time, or interpretations thereof, produced three seasons of 120 days that were split into four monthly periods of thirty days.

- At some point before the fourth dynasty, five extra days were added, bringing the total number to 365.

- The event that was chosen to secure the calendar to was the appearance/rising of what is referred to as the Dog Star, Sirius. The Kemites called this star Sopdet.

- Sopdet (Sirius) made an appearance every year at dawn, around the same time, at a specific latitude (Montet, 1964).

- The Sopdet (Sothis) year coincided with the true or year we follow today; with a very slight miscalculation.

  - The error was so small that it would have to have been scientifically analyzed for an extended period of time before the mistake would have been caught.

cc. Doctors, veterinary surgeons, fisherman, hunters, farmers, and so on, all utilized the seasonal calendar.

- Doctors in Kmt knew that there were particular diseases which appeared or were more frequent during certain times of the year.

- Some medicinal prescriptions were written during the first two months of a season, while others were written during the last two. Others yet could be used throughout the entire year.

dd. Being very sharp astronomers, the Kemites were able to tell the difference between (Montet, 1964):

- Imperishable stars (circumpolar- around or near a pole on earth stars)

- Indefatigable stars (stars that are untiring)

- Planets

- Stars that were not visible at all hours of the night.

ee. The Kemites discovered truth north using stellar observation.

- The Memphite pyramids, specifically noting the Great Pyramid, were all situated with pin point accuracy.

- This level of accuracy was not possible when utilizing the flow of the Hapi (Nile) or from analyzing the rising/setting of the sun. Kemetic scientists had to have been conducting astronomical observations (Montet, 1964).

ff. The Kemites were not only interested in their own history, geography, and chief exports but that of neighboring countries and cultures as well.

- This may explain the documentation of important data on each *sepat* (nome) of Kmt in administrative offices, and inscriptions on temple walls.

  - Some of the details included were (Montet, 1964):

    - First the name of the *sepat* (nome), chief town, secondary cult center, river or canal, agricultural lands, pehu (borders) in which flood water from the Hapi collects, land surface area

- The Punt colonnade and the Libyan bas-reliefs at Deir-el-Bahari and on the temple of Sahure respectively provide evidence that the Kemites were very knowledgeable about the phenotypes, cultural clothing, and the plants and animals of their neighboring countries.

gg. Kmt was widely known during antiquity for having very knowledgeable physicians.

- Doctors in Kmt were often the priests of Sekhmet, who was the goddess of epidemics.

hh. Our current knowledge of Kemetic medicine comes from the different papyri, such as:

- Edwin Smith Surgical Papyrus , Ebers Papyrus, and Hearst Papyrus

ii. The Kemites were able to identify the difference between trauma that is caused by a fall, a strong impact (punch or blow), disease or an accident of some type (Montet, 1964).

- The Kemites knew that dirt was partly responsible for the spread of disease since keeping one's body and home clean were highly encouraged.

- Castor oil was a very useful treatment option in Kmt and the text written on its healing properties in the Ebers Papyrus can be compared with the best chapters in the surgical papyrus (Montet, 1964).

jj. In the various fields of science, specialists documented extensive amounts of facts for:

- Supplying information to government officials

- Travelers and technicians

- Easing the suffering of the sick or injured.

A. BOTHWELL GOSSE

BRIEF AUTHOR BIO

- Authored The Knights Templars & The Magic of the Pyramids and the Mystery of the Sphinx

- Was initiated into the Masonic order at Lodge #6 in London.

- Studied a multitude of topics in England, including Egyptology.

- Was a violinist and pianist

Sources:
vrijmetselaarsgilde.eu/Maconnieke%20Encyclopedie/Franc-M/fra-b-03.htm#13
isfdb.org/cgi-bin/ea.cgi?37343

THE CIVILIZATION OF THE ANCIENT EGYPTIANS

MANUSCRIPT TYPE: Book

Main Points from the Text:

a. In Kmt, everyone is taught at least the three R's: reading, writing, and (a)rithmetic.

   ■ It is at age four that the children of Kmt are able to begin becoming a "writer in the house of books." (Gosse, 1915, p. 14)

b. Writing was the foundation of Kemetic education, just as reading is at the foundation of European/Western education.

- Children in Kmt who were taught writing had a daily quota of three pages to copy for practice.

c. Kemetic children were taught mathematics through the various games that they learned to play (Gosse, 1915; Plato, 1892).

d. A full the elementary curriculum included Kemetic children learning swimming, sacred songs, and dances as well.

- A special emphasis was placed on a student's manners and morals too (Gosse, 1915).

e. The ending time of the Kemetic school day was around noon.

f. A strict code of discipline was enforced as students were expected to never waste time, and to keep busy with their studies.

g. In addition to their elementary school education, Kemetic boys were taught their father's line of work.

- Those children who were chosen for scholarly positions continued on to university.

- Some Kemetic children attended schools related to specific civil service positions (Gosse, 1915).

h. The favored position or occupation of Kemetic students was the scribe due to the opportunities available to those individuals.

i. There was a school just for seshu (scribes) connected to the (Royal) Court (Gosse, 1915).

- Students that entered the school taught with the children of royals, regardless of their caste.

j. All children who went on to become soldiers or entered the Kemetic military received the same education.

- To ascend the ranks of the military, Kemetic children needed to receive some sort of a scholarly education.

k. There were two types of education systems present in Kmt (Gosse, 1915).

- The first known education system involved Kemetic students being trained for specialized careers in departmental schools from childhood.

- In the second system Kemetic children began at the elementary writing schools, and afterward would continue on to a university.

l. Curricula used in the Kemetic universities were very extensive. Some of the subject covered included:

- Writing (both Hieroglyphic and Hieratic), geography, cosmography, astronomy, geometry (both practical and theoretical), surveying, architecture, sculpture and painting, ritual dancing and music, law, and medicine (Gosse, 1915, p. 18).

m. There were several centers of learning, with each of them being distinguished or specializing in a particular subject area.

- The great religious or priestly college was at Khmunu (Hermopolis to the Greeks).

- This college was also the center of theoretical studies, with applied sciences being studied at Ineb-hedj/Men-nefer and Ann (Gosse, 1915).

n. Great strides were made in dentistry in Kmt, as evidence of the teeth of mummies that were very precisely repaired with gold.

o. In almost every instance, the positions of gynecologists were filled by women.

p. Medical students were not able to study or practice in more than one specific area (Gosse, 1915).

q. The courts of the temples were always crowded with travelers from foreign lands who wanted to experience the majesty of Kmt's libraries and extremely thorough scientific training.

   - Speaking of the foreigners entering Kmt to receive their education:

"Thales of Miletus received his education in science here [Kmt]... Ctesibus who invented the force-pump; and Hero, the pioneer of the steam-engine, came to Egypt for instructions in mechanics..."

She continued:

"Hypatia... studied there, and... rose to fame as a lecturer...Archimedes...was a very young man when he arrived...there he learned the fundamental principles on which his inventions were based" (Gosse, 1915, p.20).

DR. BOB BRIER
&
A. HOYT HOBBS

Brief Author Bio

- Author, Egyptologist & Senior Research Fellow – Long Island University

- Has written several books including *Cleopatra's Needles* & *Egyptomania*

- Received his Ph.D. - UNC

- Hoyt Hobbs is Prof. of Philosophy – Long Island University

- Authored other titles, such as *Fielding's Complete Guide to Egypt*

Sources:
drbobbrier.com/about-bob-brier
en.wikipedia.org/wiki/Bob_Brier
amazon.com/Ancient-Egypt-Everyday-Life-Land/dp/1454909072

DAILY LIFE
OF THE
ANCIENT EGYPTIANS

MANUSCRIPT TYPE: Book

Main Points from the Text:

a. Concerning medicine and mathematics, Brier and Hobbs maintained:

> "Physics, chemistry and biology were never studied by ancient Egyptians since true science with its controlled experiments, careful observations and testable results did not exist until long after their early, superstitious times."

Brier and Hobbs continued:

> "Still, Egyptians approached injuries and diseases more objectively than their contemporaries, and mathematics,

essential for the complex and precise buildings that Egyptians erected, was taught in every school" (Brier & Hobbs, 2008, p. 271).

b. While the Kemites did have specialists for many medical problems, they did not have any specialists in dentistry. Individuals with dental problems of any kind would have had to just live with it.

- Since dental infections happened so often, and with bad breath being socially offenseive the Kemites developed the world's first known breath mints (Brier & Hobbs, 2008).

  - These mints were made of a blend of frankincense, myrrh, and cinnamon that was then boiled with honey and molded into small round balls (Brier & Hobbs, 2008).

c. When it comes to the administering of medical treatment, the Kemites had two different methods: clinical and magical.

- Kemetic physicians would use the clinical approach:

  "As long as the cause of a medical problem was known to Egyptians, as in the case of broken bones and crocodile bites, they treated it in a clinical manner..."

  Kemetic physicians would use the magical approach:

  "If, however, the affliction was something like a fever whose cause was unknown, it was attributed to demons or malicious magic and treated with magical cures" (Brier & Hobbs, 2008, p. 273)

d. The Edwin Smith papyrus is suspected by some scholars to have been written by Imhotep due to its age.

- The author of this medical text described trauma cases that were untreatable, such as severe head trauma where the patient is unconscious as if they were there to observe firsthand these injuries.

e. The meninges (material covering the brain) were referred to as *nt-nt* (netenet) by Kemetic doctors.

- The vocabulary used by the writer referred to a material like an animal skin, and the meninges is a type of skin covering (Brier & Hobbs, 2008).

- Even with all of the progress made in understanding the brain and its function in the human body, Kmt never had any brain specialists.

f. Kemetic doctors traveled with troops during times of war and were in positions to analyze organs and bones while treating them.

g. Due to the lack of training and being toward the lower end of the social ladder in Kmt, embalmers were in no position to contribute anything to Kemetic medical knowledge (Brier & Hobbs, 2008).

h. Many ingredients used by Kemetic doctors have been proven to have medicinal uses today.

- Ground malachite was recommended for patients with open wounds. Malachite contains a substance called cupric carbonate, which when tested, has been found to kill certain infectious bacteria, for example staphylococcus (Brier & Hobbs, 2008).

- Honey was another very ingredient that was frequently used by Kemetic doctors, and that has been shown to kill bacteria as well.

i. Herodotus had the following to say about specialized medicine in Kmt:

"The practice of medicine they split up into separate parts, each doctor being responsible for the treatment of only one disease. There are...innumerable doctors, some specializing in diseases of the eyes...the head...the teeth...the stomach and so on" (Brier & Hobbs, 2008, p.283).

j. Kemetic mathematical expertise extended only to addition and subtraction; not division or multiplication due to never developing a theoretical understanding of numbers.

- Multiplication in Kmt was achieved by what is referred to as the 'Method of Doubling'.

- The Kemites only used 1 as a numerator for fractions.

k. The Kemites developed the 365-day-year, as well as the 24-hour day.

- They did this by dividing the night and day into 12 hours each.

DR. MARSHALL CLAGETT

BRIEF AUTHOR BIO

- Received his Ph.D. – Columbia University

- Served as Prof. –History & Science – University of Wisconsin

- Prof. Emer.– Princeton University

- Authored a five volume work on Archimedes during the Middle Ages

---

Sources:

telegraph.co.uk/news/obituaries/1501628/Marshall-Clagett.html

ias.edu/scholars/marshall-clagett

ANCIENT EGYPTIAN SCIENCE VOL. II & III

MANUSCRIPT TYPE: Book

Main Points from the Text:

a. The 365 day calendar was already completed and in place by the time of the Old Kingdom (ca. 2665 B.C.E.).

b. Clagett gave a breakdown of the 365 day or civil calendar:

> *"...the civil year consisted of twelve months of thirty days each plus 5 epagomenal days (days inserted at certain periods of time), totaling 365 days. The months were grouped in three seasons of four months each..."* (Clagett, 1995, p. 4).

c. For the early Kemites, day and night was divided into 12 hours each according to the seasons.

- The Pyramid Texts provides evidence of how day and night was separated in the following translated quotes:

  - "Oh you who are over the hours, who are before Re, prepare a way for Wenis."

  - "Wenis has cleared the night; Wenis has dispatched the hours" (Clagett, 1995, p. 49).

d. The earliest known examples of mathematical quantifying in ancient Kmt came in the form of counting various items, such as possessions, captives or slaves, and so forth.

e. Being able to count successive years resulted in the ability of the Kemites to measure the length of a per-Aa's reign (Clagett, 1999).

f. mdu nTr numerals can be found on artifacts as early as the "predynastic" Scorpion mace-head as well as the Palermo stone.

g. The Kemites used different units of measurement (Clagett, 1999).

- *mh-ni-swt/meh-ni-sut* (royal cubit), and was around 52.3cm or 20.6 inches. The royal cubit was used for smaller lengths.

- *mh-Snt/meh-shent* (100 cubits) was used for measurements of fields.

- *Ater/itr* was known as the 'river measure,' and is equal to 20,000 cubits, and was about 10.5 km. It was the longest unit of measure used for large fields.

h. Kemetic scholars developed many mathematical concepts, such as the concept of arithmetic, approximating fractions, and geometric progressions.

- The Reisner Papyri shows how Kemetic scholars practiced the approximation of fractions.

- Kemetic mathematicians also created math puzzles present in the Rhind Papyrus, according to Dr. Danesi of the University of Toronto.

i. The following is a list of six mathematical papyri and the dates that were thought to be developed in Kmt (Clagett, 1999):

- Rhind Papyrus (ca. 1844 – 1797 B.C.E.).

- Moscow Mathematical Papyrus (ca. 1783 – 1640 B.C.E.).

- Kahun Mathematical Papyrus (Later part of the Twelfth Dynasty).

- Berlin Papyrus (Later part of the Twelfth Dynasty through the Thirteenth Dynasty).

- Mathematical Leather Roll – British Museum (Seventeenth century B.C.E.).

- Reisner Papyrus I (ca. 1991 – 1786 B.C.E.).

DR. WILL DURANT

BRIEF AUTHOR BIO

- Author & Historian

- Received his Ph.D. –
Columbia University

- Also authored *The Story of Philosophy*

- Was Dir. of Labor Temple School - NY

Sources:

The Story of Civilization

nytimes.com/1981/11/09/obituaries/historian-will-durant-dies-author-of-civilization-series.html

THE STORY OF CIVILIZATION: OUR ORIENTAL HERITAGE VOL. I

MANUSCRIPT TYPE: Book

Main Points from the Text:

a. Champollion's decipherment of the mdu nTr resulted in the discovery of Kmt's alphabet.

b. From the very outset of recorded Kemetic history, highly developed and advanced mathematics could be found (Durant, 1963).

  - The design of the pyramids that involved a precise measurement was not possible without a considerable mathematical tradition.

- Nearly all the ancient writers agree when they ascribed the invention of geometry to the Kemites.

- Of Kemetic geometry, Durant stated the following:

  "Egyptian geometry measured not only the area of squares, circles, and cubes, but also the cubic content of cylinders and spheres..." (Durant, 1963, p. 180)

- The concepts of Kemetic multiplication and division are as old as the pyramids (Durant, 1963).

c. Life in Kmt was dependent on the flooding of the Hapi, as such; it led to very careful calculations of the Hapi's rise and fall.

- This constant measuring and re-measuring was considered the beginning of geometry.

d. The priests delivered a primary education to the well-to-do Kemetic children in schools that were built onto the temples themselves.

e. Within the ruins of a school that was supposedly a part of the Ramesseum, a large quantity of shells were discovered that still had lesson materials written on them, apparently from the students of the school (Durant, 1963).

f. The role of teachers in Kmt was to continually train seshu (scribes) to take positions within the government.

g. Once the Hieratic and Demotic scripts were developed, writing became more widespread amongst the general public.

h. Regarding Kemetic literature, Durant (1963) proclaimed that:

> *"Short stories are diverse and plentiful in the fragments that have come down to us of Egyptian literature"* (p. 175).

- The oldest known form of the Cinderella story was written in Kmt.

i. The scholars of Kmt proclaimed that the first known sciences were developed around 18,000 B.C.E. (Durant, 1963).

j. The Kemites' Mesopotamian neighbors were more advanced in terms of science education and research.

k. Perhaps the Kemites were not publishing everything that they knew on the sciences as a means of protecting information sacred to them and as a result, they were hesitant to share it (Durant, 1963).

l. For countless centuries the Kemites were recording the positions and paths of the planets.

- The Kemites could tell the difference between objects in the sky that were planets and those that were stars.

- The Kemites were recording fifth magnitude stars that are, according to Harvard University's Astronomical Magnitude Scale (n.d.), the faintest visible stars to the naked eye in dark rural areas.

- The fact that the Kemites could see such stars makes sense, given their physical environment and unobstructed view of the skies (Durant, 1963).

m. The Kemites showed that from observing the heavens for many millennia, they were able build the calendar.

- The year was divided into three seasons that contained four months in each and thirty days in each month (Durant, 1963).

  - The first season was the inundation and recession of the Hapi called *Akhet*.

  - The second season was the period of cultivation or appearance of crops called *Peret*.

  - The third season was the period of harvesting or summertime called *Shemu*.

  - Thirty days were used to each month due to it being the most suitable calculation for the lunar month of twenty-nine and half days.

■ Durant (1963) called the calendar another of Kmt's great contributions to mankind.

n. The oldest known clock in human history is dated back to the reign of Thutmose III (Durant, 1963).

THE STORY OF CIVILIZATION: THE LIFE OF GREECE VOL. II

MANUSCRIPT TYPE: Book

Main Points from the Text:

a. Thales of Miletus learned geometry, among other subjects, from teachers in Kmt.

b. Rhoecus, and his son, Theodurs; both Greek sculptors during the sixth century B.C.E., learned how to create hollowed casts made of bronze in Kmt (Durant, 1966).

c. As Greece was experiencing social and philosophical crises, Plato became admittedly jealous of the sacred tradition and the strength of the stability of the philosophical so-called religious thought in Kmt (Durant, 1966).

d. Eudoxus spent at least 16 months studying astronomy with the priests in the Kemetic city of On (Heliopolis to the Greeks).

e. Greek mathematics owed its stimulus and development to the scholarly priests of ancient Kmt.

   ▪ While the Greek arts and writing were deteriorating, Greek science was reaching its zenith during the Hellenistic age (ca. 323 – 30 B.C.E.) due in part to its contact with Kmt (Durant, 1966).

      • Kemetic medical literature fueled breakthroughs and developments in Greek medicine during the Hellenistic age.

f. The so-called *"Fathers of Medicine"* in Greece made few to no advances in at all on the medical knowledge and practices developed by physicians in Kmt a millennium before (Durant, 1966).

- Particularly, as it concerned specialized areas of medicine, the development of Greek medicine had failed to compare to Kmt

- The oppression, expulsion, imprisonment, and overall mistreatment of Greece's great thinkers, such as Anaxagoras, Socrates, Aspasia, and others, resulted in very little progress if any being made in Greek science.

g. Siphons had been used in Kmt as far back as 1500 B.C.E., which Greek inventor, Ctesibius, studied in Alexandria some 1,700 years later.

h. Greek mathematician and scholar, Archimedes, most likely enhanced and *accidentally* put his name to the Kemetic water screw (Durant, 1966).

- The Kemetic water screw, misnamed Archimedes' screw, is a device that was first used ca. 2,000 years ago in Kmt for moving water up from low bodies of water for purpose of irrigation

PLATO

Brief Author Bio

- Was a student of Socrates Philosopher & Author

- Thought to have written at least 36 dialogues & writings

- Philosopher & Author

- Well-known writings include the Republic

- Is credited with several philosophical doctrines, such as the Nous (World Soul), that originated in ancient Egypt

---

Sources:

Stolen Legacy

britannica.com/biography/Plato

THE DIALOGUES OF PLATO: LAWS VOL. II

MANUSCRIPT TYPE: Book

Main Points from the Text:

a. Three academic subjects were appropriate or suitable for free Greek citizens to take up or pursue: arithmetic, geometry, astronomy.

b. In book seven, Plato exclaimed that all free people and children of free people [speaking of Greeks] should learn as much about arithmetic, geometry, and astronomy, as the Kemetic child knows or is taught (Plato, 1892).

    ▪ Arithmetic was woven into the games played by the Kemetic children. Kemetic teachers would arrange various objects such that the students would have to perform basic calculations.

- Kemetic teachers taught ordinal numbers by arranging students who participated in physical activities in a certain order. By doing so, students were able to understand how their turns came in numerical order.

- In describing the "swinish" or pig like ignorance of the people of Greece, Plato announced to his friend Cleinias:

  "... I, like yourself, have late in life heard with amazement of our ignorance in these matters ;... we appear to be more like pigs than men, and I am quite ashamed, not only of myself, but of all Hellenes" (Plato, 1892, p. 202).

c. Learning arithmetic was the strongest possible educational tool that can be used to shape the minds of young students.

- However, it awakens in those who learn it, a rudeness of character. Along with making the individual quick to learn; not to mention it darkened the character.

  - The Kemites and Phoenicians were said to have developed the rudeness of character mentioned (Plato, 1892).

d. Several millennia ago, the Kemites understood that they had to instill the concepts of honor and integrity in their young people (Plato, 1892).

  - In their artistic expressions, whether it was music, dance (both of which were a part of the Kemetic education curricula), the ideas of honor and integrity were evident.

e. The Greeks sought to do just as the Kemites did, and add an element of sacredness to their various forms of dancing and singing.

f. The social and political stability of Kmt's educational and religious systems greatly impressed the Greeks, especially that of Plato.

DR. ROSALIE DAVID

BRIEF AUTHOR BIO

- Received her Ph.D. – University of Liverpool

- Prof. Emer. – University of Manchester

- Fmr. Dir. – International Mummy Database

- First woman to become Prof. of Egyptology in Britain

- Authored a number of titles on ancient Egyptian religion like *A Guide to Religious Ritual at Abydos*

Sources:
ees.ac.uk/faqs/rosalie-david
en.wikipedia.org/wiki/Ann_Rosalie_David

HANDBOOK TO LIFE IN ANCIENT EGYPT

MANUSCRIPT TYPE: Book

Main Points from the Text:

a. The complex feat of regulating the Hapi (Nile) was a process that started with Per-Aa Scorpion. Dam building and irrigation are complex sciences that must have been thoroughly developed.

b. Kmt's main produce was cereals, and the knowledge of how to grow cereals was received from the Near East (David, 2003).

c. The exact date of when mdu nTr was initially created is unknown due in part to how old it is. However, it is known that by 3100 B.C.E., mdu nTr was already a completely developed language and writing.

d. The Kemetic language went through three stages of development: Hieratic, Demotic, and finally, Coptic.

e. There were various types of libraries in Kmt: private and town libraries and temple libraries.

- Those in Kmt who kept personal libraries often kept their papyri in jars or boxes (David, 2003).

  - Private libraries were discovered in Waset (Thebes/Luxor).

  - The papyri often consisted of documents necessary for completing daily tasks (David, 2003).

- Temple libraries often kept literary, religious, and scientific papyri.

f. Temples were often institutions of higher learning in Kmt. Priests were responsible for a plethora of subjects, such as: Public worship, astronomy, and astrology (David, 2003).

- The Ramesseum in Waset was determined to have been used as a school.

g. Sacred writings were developed and housed in the per-ankh, as well as lessons being taught there.

- In addition, medical, magical, and religious texts were developed and copied in these places.

h. The temple of Seti I in Aabdju (Abydos) had a specific room with spaces or cubby holes in which they kept scrolls and other important educational documents.

i. Boys, as well as girls, no matter their social status, received an education in Kmt.

"The Egyptian system of education is not clearly defined in the papyri, but it seems that most children, boys and girls, whatever their social status, received some kind of education up to a certain age" (David, 2003, p. 250).

- Up to the age of 4 the mothers were responsible for teaching the children. After which, the father took up the responsibility and continued their education.

- Some of the boys in Kmt went to schools within their hometown, while others went to schools and received training specific to their trade or profession.

j. Education in Kmt was not free, and families were expected to offer payment for their children's education (David, 2003).

- In rural areas, the particular produce of those areas were given as payment.

k. The Kemetic school curriculum attempted to mold a student into a person who possessed scientific/scholarly traits but also one who also displayed self-control, manners, and morals.

- This curriculum was designed to make a person more well-rounded or complete, and was repeatedly praised and talked about by the Greeks (David, 2003).

l. At age 14, young men were educated in their father's occupation, while it was unlikely that girls continued their education beyond the elementary type of education.

m. Credit for the earliest known wisdom teachings belong to the sage Hardedef of the Old Kingdom period (ca. 2665 – 2160 B.C.E.) from which the foundation of education lessons in Kmt.

n. The point of education, among other things was to establish an upper class. This upper class of Kemites were responsible for looking after the interests of the lower class:

> "Education was used to create an elite class, but the scribes... were also expected to exercise the highest standards of behavior and to protect with impartiality the interests of the weak and less fortunate" (David, 2003, p. 253).

o. The Greeks considered the ancient Kemites extremely skilled in mathematics and astronomy.

p. Kemetic astronomers were able to distinguish between imperishable stars (circumpolar stars) and indefatigable stars (stars and planets not visible at all hours of the night) (David, 2003).

- Stellar observations were used by the Kemites to determine true north, as well as situate the pyramids with incredible accuracy.

q. The Kemites became convinced that the earth was flat and was thus floating in the middle of an ocean the shape of a circle.

r. Kemetic physicians were able to create balanced and sensible treatments from patient examinations and a solid understanding of anatomy

- These treatments in part came from the development of the mummification process.

s. Abstract mathematical thought is rarely ever attributed to the Kemites, and yet they were able to construct the pyramids, for example.

- Kemetic mathematics was very awkward and crude but they were able to, for example, make careful and meticulous measurements.

- Rather than rely on the usage of reasoning in mathematics, the Kemites instead leaned on functional experiences (David, 2003).

JOHN D. BALDWIN

BRIEF AUTHOR BIO

- Politician, Minister & Writer on anthropology

- Received honorary Master's degree – Yale University

- Graduated from Yale Divinity School

- Fmr. member of the American Oriental Society

- Author of other anthropological titles, such as *Ancient America in Notes on American Archaeology*

Sources: en.wikipedia.org/wiki/John_Denison_Baldwin

PRE-HISTORIC NATIONS

MANUSCRIPT TYPE: Book

Main Points from the Text:

a. Greeks visited Kmt toward the end of what was called the New Monarchy or New Kingdom period (Baldwin, 1874).

- It was during this period that the Greeks studied in the schools of Kmt.

- In addition to the schools that the Greeks had access to, they also made use of the libraries and closely studied various monuments around Kmt.

- They also had access to an abundance of Kemetic knowledge and information as far as written material was concerned.

- The Greeks were more likely to plagiarize or steal Kemetic scientific and philosophical ideas without citing that they got the ideas from Kmt.

  - Herodotus often spoke openly of all that the Greeks received from the Kemites in terms of cultural, philosophical, and scientific thought. Several scholars, such as J. A. S. Evans, have severely criticized Herodotus for distorting truth and telling lies (Evans, 1968; Roberts, 2017).

b. Sir Gardner Wilkinson is cited as stating that the Kemites were in possession of a superb mathematical understanding during the time of Menes (ca. 3100 B.C.E.) (Baldwin, 1874).

  - The evidence given to support this was the fact that Menes had the flow of the Hapi (Nile) altered; a feat that had to be researched very carefully.

c. Karl Lepsius described the creation of the Kemetic writing systems. Lepsius explained how the writing systems of the Kemites were able to capture all of the various stages that human writing goes through (ideographical signs, syllables, and sounds represented by the use of consonants and vowels), which meant that the Kemetic writing systems had to have gone through a lengthy development period (Baldwin, 1874; Lepsius, 1849).

d. As far as the writing system of Kmt was concerned:

> "In no other old nation of which we have sufficient knowledge to form an opinion on this point was the art of writing so perfect or so largely used as in Egypt, especially for memorial and historical purposes" (Baldwin, 1874, p. 300).

e. The Kemites appeared to have had literary works as numerous as the inscriptions of mdu nTr on the temples of Kmt.

- The concept of a library had to have been established quite early on in Kmt's history (Baldwin, 1874).

f. Diodorus Siculus, and stated that there existed a great library of Ramses II (The Great). The rooms of this library, according to Diodorus, were located in the temple of Ramses II at Waset (Thebes) (Baldwin, 1874; Siculus, 1989).

g. The tombs of two librarians; Nebnufre (father) and Nufrehetep (son), were discovered in Waset (Baldwin, 1874).

- They were librarians during the rule of Ramses II (The Great), which in terms of chronology, increased the likelihood that the father and son were the same librarians described by Diodorus centuries ago.

- The Kemites were long aware of the use and idea of libraries; that books, and the collecting of them, were certainly older than Menes.

h. When Solon journeyed to Kmt, he met a priest in Sau (Sais), who spoke about the Greeks and a knowledge of history. According to accounts by both Solon and Plato the priest stated:

> "*You Greeks are novices in knowledge of antiquity. You are ignorant of what passed, either here or among yourselves...8,000 [sic] years is deposited in our sacred books; but I can...tell you what our fathers have done for 9,000 [sic] years...*" (Baldwin, 1874, p. 302; Plato, 1888).

Solon and Plato both have maintained that what the priest said above to Solon is probable, and could find no reason to dispute the accounts.

DR. REGINE SCHULZ

&

DR. MATTHIAS SEIDEL

BRIEF AUTHOR BIO

- Dr. Schulz is Snr. Dir. –
  Roemer and Pelizaeus
  Museum – Hildesheim,
  Germany

- Prof. – Institute of
  Egyptology & Coptology-
  LMU - Munich

- Dr. Seidel studied
  Egyptology, Middle
  Eastern archaeology &
  Classical archaeology

- Taught at a number of
  universities in Europe &
  North America

Sources:

aegyptologie.uni-muenchen.de/personen/apl_professoren/schulz/index.html
de.wikipedia.org/wiki/Regine_Schulz
aucpress.com/product/precious-egypt-4/

EGYPT:
THE WORLD OF
THE PHARAOHS

MANUSCRIPT TYPE: Book

Main Points from the Text:

a. Prior to the dynastic periods, early Kemites were already showing economic forethought with examples, such as smoking and drying fish (Schulz & Seidel, 2004).

   ▪ Kilns were also present that were used for drying grains, which shows the developing of food storing techniques.

b. Copper ores were being used in pre-dynastic Kmt. Most likely they were being utilized as a dye in the production of cosmetics.

c. Kemites in pre-dynastic Upper Kmt used special firing techniques when creating pottery.

  - Furnaces were being used to create ceramic items that required high levels of skill (Schulz & Seidel, 2004).

d. Workshops were found where stones were being hollowed out and polished in decorative ways.

e. The mdu nTr (hieroglyphs) found on vessels in Kmt date back to pre-dynastic times (Naqada III – ca. 3300/3200 B.C.E.) (Schulz & Seidel, 2004).

f. The Kemites carried out nationwide censuses for the purpose of collecting taxes. This census was connected to a ritual called Followers of Heru (Horus).

g. Ship building was a necessary skill for trading and other endeavors during the Old Kingdom period (ca. 2665 – 2160 B.C.E.).

- Timber had to be imported from the Levant (a region in Asia), in particular, Byblos, and brought into Kmt for shipbuilding among other things.

h. Calculations put the number of workers needed to build the pyramids of Giza at 20,000 – 25,000 (Schulz & Seidel, 2004).

- The specialists working on the pyramids were: quarrymen, stonemasons, sappers, carriers, bricklayers, plasterers, food servers, engineers, architects.

i. As to the advent of writing in Kmt:

"According to artifacts recently unearthed...in Cairo, the date of the origin of writing in Egypt has been adjusted earlier by several centuries. Until now this time frame was assumed to have been around 3000 B.C.E." (Schulz & Seidel, 2004, p. 343)

j. The mdu nTr in a sense suddenly appeared in Kmt as a complete system that remained relatively unchanged for over 3,500 years (Schulz & Seidel, 2004).

k. The papyrus plant was thought to be a better choice, rather than using stone or clay for writing in Kmt.

l. The Kemites often used black and red ink. Black ink was created with soot, and red ink with ochre or hematite (Schulz & Seidel, 2004).

- Red ink was used to start new chapters, dates, and like today, and also checking a student's work to perform corrections.

m. In learning to write, students in scribal schools copied picture words as complete pieces rather than sign by sign or piece by piece.

n. There were some Kemites who sought out and collected books simply because of their love for writing and literature.

- These libraries were grown and then passed down within the family to future generations (Schulz & Seidel, 2004).

o. The number and type of topics that were written about in Kemetic texts and literature are just about the same as those still being studied today.

p. Due to the nature of their jobs, there was a very high literacy rate in the village of Deir el-Medineh. There were a multitude of texts written about everyday life by many of those who lived there.

q. The training and rearing of the children during their early developmental years were more often than not the responsibility of the mother.

  - If the child/children were boys, from a certain age they were raised then by their fathers, who trained their son's to follow in their footsteps.

  - If the child/children chose a profession different from the father, they were sent to a school for that particular profession and they were taught to read, write, and do arithmetic (Schulz & Seidel, 2004).

r. Herodotus' explanation of the embalming techniques used by the Kemites was incredibly precise as recent investigations of mummies today have confirmed (Schulz & Seidel, 2004).

- Some scholars suspect that Herodotus personally saw how Kemetic embalming specialists went through the embalming process take place during his time spent in Kmt.

s. Kemetic embalmers developed their own blends of resinous liquids to be poured into the skulls after removing the brain (Schulz & Seidel, 2004).

- A chemical analysis revealed that the liquids consisted of resins from coniferous trees, bee's wax, and aromatic plant oils.

DR. ALY SABER M.D.

BRIEF AUTHOR BIO

- Consultant surgeon & Gen. Mgr. – Port-Fouad General Hospital

- Faculty of Medicine – Suez Canal University - Egypt

- Authored or Co-authored as many as 70 publications

Sources:
linkedin.com/in/aly-saber-7a1b9466/
researchgate.net/profile/Aly_Saber

ANCIENT EGYPTIAN SURGICAL HERITAGE

MANUSCRIPT TYPE: Book

Main Points from the Text:

a. Homer stated that medicine was without a doubt, the most famous of all of the sciences studied in Kmt.

b. The medical papyri and texts supply solid evidence about surgeons and surgery in Kmt. There was, in fact, no doubt that a mature and advanced medical profession existed within Kmt, specifically, the role of surgeon.

c. As the profession of doctor in Kmt had an established "pecking order", the following are some of the Kemetic terms for titles in the field of medicine in Kmt (Saber, 2010, p. 328):

- *Wr-swnw* or ur-sunu (Senior Doctors)

- *Swnw* or sunu (Junior doctors)

- *Imy-r-swnw* or imy-r-sunu (Doctors)

- *Smsw-swnw* or shem-sunu (Registrar's)

- *Shd-swnw* or shed-sunu (Consultants)

d. Several references were made in medical papyri to medical tools used by the Kemites. Some examples of these tools include:

- Surgical knives, drills, saws, hooks, forceps, pinchers, scales, spoons, probes, catheters, and so on (Saber, 2010).

  - Many of these tools are used today, and that use was made possible in large part or completely due to Kemetic ingenuity.

e. The ancient Kemites also knew of suturing. The first known documented case of suturing came to us from the Edwin Smith papyrus (Saber, 2010).

- Written accounts from between ca. 1600 and 1000 B.C.E. revealed that the Kemites, as well as the Harappan people of ancient India, were using flax seed and hemp in the suturing process.

f. The Kemites were no strangers to making medical incisions either. For example, they used the phrase *at nt ryt* and *at nt whdw* to refer to opening abscesses (Saber, 2010).

  - The Kemites also used *at nt dj* to refer to removing a fatty tumor.

g. Kemetic surgeons used blades that were heated to approximately 690 - 745°C (965 - 1020°K) before making incisions.

  - This was done to cut and almost simultaneously be able to seal the wound and curb bleeding as well (Saber, 2010).

h. The process of cauterizing a wound is said to have been first explained by Kemetic medical professionals in the Ebers papyrus (Saber, 2010).

i. The Ebers and Edwin Smith papyri revealed that Kemitic physicians were the first known medical professionals to document and record medicinal practice in a very methodical fashion.

j. Kemetic physicians were conducting physical examinations as early as 5,000 years ago (Saber, 2010; Stiefel, Shaner, & Schaefer, 2006).

   ▪ These examinations included being questioned by the physician to try and determine the cause of the illness.

k. Physicians in Kmt began their diagnosis of patients by uttering the words, "Thou should say concerning him [the patient]... ," and it would end with one of the three following statements (Saber, 2010, p. 330):

   ▪ An ailment that I will treat.

- An ailment with which I will contend.

- An ailment not to be treated.

l. Due to its mathematical significance, the Eye of Heru (Horus) was used by Kemetic physicians to, among other things, to produce medicines.

m. Evidence is present in the Smith Papyrus that shows that Kemetic medical professionals did perform dissections on humans (Saber, 2010).

CLAUDIA ZASLAVSKY
(CONTRIBUTOR)

BRIEF AUTHOR BIO

- Educator & Ethno-mathematician

- Was a proponent of multicultural mathematics being taught in schools

- Also author of *Africa Counts*

- Studied mathematics – Hunter College & University of Michigan

---

Sources:
aalbc.com/authors/
en.wikipedia.org/wiki/Claudia_Zaslavsky

BLACKS IN SCIENCE: ANCIENT AND MODERN

MANUSCRIPT TYPE: Book

Main Points from the Text:

a. The earliest known records of the solar year had its beginnings in Kmt several thousand years ago; even earlier in Mesopotamia (Van Sertima, 1998; Zaslavsky, 1999).

b. Wherever calendars of antiquity are being discussed, the topic of astronomy arises. In Kmt, it was the cattle herdsmen and farmers who had to watch closely the progression of the days and seasons to know when to do their respective jobs. The scholarly priests in Kmt took that knowledge from the herdsmen and farmers, and formulated it into scientific and religious thought.

The observations made by the scholarly priests over a period of several centuries allowed for them to be able to predict the arrival of the seasons and movements of celestial bodies.

- Early Greek astronomers embraced the Kemetic civil calendar and began using it as their own (Van Sertima, 1998; Zaslavsky, 1999).

c. Due to the annual flooding of the Hapi River the Kemites had a need for the development of mathematics.

d. Private land ownership and the trading of various products created a need for the development of mathematics in the form of weights and measures (Van Sertima, 1998; Zaslavsky, 1999).

e. Mathematics was used to address various societal dilemmas in Kmt. One such example was the yearly flooding of the Hapi (Nile) river. After the Hapi flooded, the land would need to be divided again, which necessitated the need for the development and use of mathematics.

- Today's calculation of π (3.14159265359) was close to the ancient Kemetic calculation of π (3.16) (Van Sertima, 1998; Zaslavsky, 1999).

- The first earliest known examples of rectangular coordinate geometry were found in the tombs of the per-Aas astronomical texts that revealed how the position of the stars could tell the time of night.

  - This clock, as Zaslavsky (1999) put it, showed the times that were appropriate for temple services.

f. Ancient Kemetic scholars had created whole curricula to train others who were entering the priesthood and study. It is these same curricula that the Kemetic scholars used to educate the Greeks.

g. Once the vast libraries of Kmt were open to visitors, the Greeks no doubts had ample opportunity to write down much of what they read.

- After which, Greeks were given credit for what Kmt accomplished well before them and thus flowed to the East (Van Sertima, 1998; Zaslavsky, 1999).

DRS. KHALIL
&
GUIRGUIS MESSIHA ET AL.
(CONTRIBUTORS)

BRIEF AUTHOR BIO

- Dr. Khalil Messiha is a physician, archaeologist & parapsychologist

- Known for his re-discovery of and theory about the 'Saqqara Bird'

- Guirguis Messiha is a flight engineer

Sources: Black in Science: Ancient and Modern

BLACKS IN SCIENCE: ANCIENT AND MODERN

MANUSCRIPT TYPE: Book

Main Points from the Text:

a. Dr. Messiha investigated the ancient Kemetic engineers' work in aeronautics. His rediscovery of the monoplane model has revealed evidence that the Kemites had knowledge of flying machines during the Late Kingdom period (ca. 760 – 657 B.C.E.) in Kmt (Van Sertima, 1999).

- Concerning the design of the monoplane model, Dr. Khalil Messiha quoted flight engineer Guirguis Messiha as saying:

  "The wing section shows that the wing surface is part of an ellipse, which gives stability in flight...the body is an

aerofoil shape, which lessens the drag, a fact...
discovered after years of experimental work in
aeronautics" (Van Setima, 1999, p. 94).

- Dr. Messiha continued on to make the following
  three points (Van Sertima, 1999):

  - Whoever constructed the monoplane model also
    built many other models before achieving the level
    of craftsmanship seen in the model being
    discussed.

  - The monoplane model is a miniature
    representation of the larger original monoplane
    that Messiha said was still present in Sakkara.

  - Pa-di-Imen (Gift of Amon) is the name of the
    Kemetic engineer that invented the monoplane
    model.

b. The design of the miniature monoplane model did not
   have wings that one would expect to find on birds.

Instead, the model had wings that are just like those you would see on an aircraft (Van Sertima, 1999).

c. Michael Frenchman reported that Guirguis Messiha described the shape of the model as aerofoil, which minimizes drag effect; a fact, Frenchman added, was only recently discovered through aeronautical research (Van Sertima, 1999).

- Frenchman quoted Dr. Khalil Messiha as saying:

   "This is no toy model... It is too scientifically designed and it took a lot of skill to make it. The man who did this studied bird flight very carefully" (Van Sertima, 1999, p. 99).

- Frenchman went further and stated that Dr. Khalil Messiha believes that the Kemites had advanced knowledge in many areas, which of course included elementary aeronautics.

BEATRICE LUMPKIN
(CONTRIBUTOR)

BRIEF AUTHOR BIO

- Member –American Association for the Advancement of Science

- Fmr. Assoc. Prof. of Mathematics – (at the now) Malcolm X College - Chicago

- Has authored/co-authored several multicultural education titles, such as *Multicultural Science and Math Connections*

Sources:
keywiki.org/Bea_Lumpkin
encyclopedia.com/arts/educational-magazines/lumpkin-beatrice-1918

BLACKS IN SCIENCE: ANCIENT AND MODERN

MANUSCRIPT TYPE: Book

Main Points from the Text:

a. The numbers that were found on the Narmer palette, dating from around the thirty-second or thirty-first century B.C.E.

  - The numbers were being used to count the cattle and prisoners depicted on the palette (Van Sertima, 1999).

b. Evidence from the International Nubian Rescue Mission revealed that mdu nTr was being used long before the ascension of Aha-Menes to the throne in Kmt.

c. In his work, *A Concise History of Mathematics*, Dirk Struik (1987), a Dutch-American mathematician and historian of mathematics, proclaimed that:

"All kinds of advanced science have been credited to the pyramid builders of 3000 B.C. and earlier years..." (p. 26).

- When Struik spoke of the adoption of the Sothic cycle (the Kemetic New Year and the sighting of Sopdet (Sirius) happening the same day; a period of approximately 1,460 years of 365 days) and development of the calendar by the Kemites, he declared:

"Such precise mathematical and astronomical work cannot be seriously ascribed to a people slowly emerging from Neolithic conditions, and the source of these tales can usually be traced to a late Egyptian tradition transmitted to us by the Greeks" (Struik, 1987, p. 26; Van Sertima, 1999, p. 100).

- Struik had not maintained a concretely Eurocentric mindset about the mathematics of the Kemites. He demonstrated the ability to look critically at the evidence regarding Kemetic mathematics:

   "As to mathematics, the Stonehenge discussions have made it necessary to rethink our ideas of what Neolithic people knew. [Professor Richard] Gillings has shown that the ancient Egyptians could work with their fractions in a most sophisticated way" (Van Sertima, 1999, p. 101).

d. Several European scholars, such as Mathematician and former Professor of Mathematics [Morris] Kline, often dismissed Kemetic mathematical science as uncivilized.

- George Sarton, an American chemist and historian, claimed:

   "It is childish to assume that science began in Greece. The 'Greek Miracle' was prepared by millennia of work in Egypt, Mesopotamia, and possibly other

regions. Greek science was less an invention than a revival" (Van Sertima, 1999, p. 101).

e. The mathematicians in Kmt contributed to all of the above by creating methods for measuring the land using specific mathematical formulas for the "areas of rectangles, triangles, circles and even the area of a curved dome" (Van Sertima, 1999, p. 102).

- The Kemites used the properties of similar triangles in combination with trigonometry to ensure that the pyramids had a constant slope.

f. The Kemites were also the only ancient civilization who had full knowledge of the correct formula for determining the volume of a truncated pyramid ($V = 1/3 (a^2 + ab + b^2) h$).

- Sources, such as physicist and encyclopedist Dr. Eric Weisstein (2018) of Wolfram MathWorld, have attributed the date of 1850 B.C.E. to this discovery.

g. Fractions were one of the most vital functions of mathematics during the time of the Kemites.

- Fractions were used to perform accounting duties for very large projects, such as building the pyramids (Van Sertima, 1999).

h. Continuing on with mathematics in Kmt, the dimensions of the Great Pyramid must be mentioned here.

- Concerning the Great Pyramid's base measurements, Lumpkin wrote that

  "The square base originally measured 755.43 ft., 755.88 ft., and 755.77 ft. on its north, south, east, and west sides respectively...".

She stated furthermore that:

"The right angles at each corner of the base, line the walls up almost perfectly with the four cardinal points" (Van Sertima, 1999, p. 71).

- To finish the discussion of the Great Pyramid, the preciseness of its base measurements and its connection to the value of π (pi) need mentioning, as Lumpkin proclaimed:

> "It is a fact that half the perimeter of the base divided by the height is 3.1408392; compared to the modern value of π of 3.1415927; a difference of only 0.0007535" (Van Sertima, 1999, p. 71).

KATHLEEN KUIPER

BRIEF AUTHOR BIO

- Fmr. Editor of the Encyclopedia Britannica

- Fmr. Editor of Merriam-Webster's Encyclopedia of Literature

- Authored other titles, such as *The Britannica Guide to Ancient Civilizations*

Sources: britannica.com/editor/Kathleen-Kuiper/6741

ANCIENT EGYPT: FROM PREHISTORY TO THE ISLAMIC CONQUEST

MANUSCRIPT TYPE: Book

Main Points from the Text:

a. The usages and the potential for writing in Kmt were dependent on and hampered by two things (Kuiper, 2011):

- What the development of writing was supposed to accomplish.

- How literate the population was.

  - Approximately ninety-nine percent of the population of Kmt was mostly likely unable to read and write.

b. The alphabet most probably comes from the mdu nTr writing system (hieroglyphs) developed in Kmt (Kuiper, 2011).

c. Land surveying was a field in which the Kemites excelled. This skill was necessary for land redistribution after the flooding of the Hapi river.

   - They had completely surveyed and established the boundaries of their country (as it were at that time) by the start of the Middle Kingdom period.

   - Redistributing the land as well as figuring out the borders of the entire nation:

     "...*required both knowledge of astronomy and highly ingenious techniques, but they apparently were achieved with little theoretical analysis*" (Kuiper, 2011, p. 23).

d. Seshu (scribes) merely supervised while everyone else worked (based on certain Kemetic texts encouraging the youth to become seshu).

e. The Kemites used data from the lengths of per-Aanic reigns and other epochs.

- Using astronomical events in connection with the three calendars t: Civil calendar, Lunar calendar, and the Solar calendar, the Kemites recorded the dates of each per-Aa's reign (Kuiper, 2011).

f. The official start to the Kemetic civil calendar began when Sopdet (Sothis to the Greeks) – the Dog Star, could be spotted in the distance on the horizon.

- This event happened just weeks prior to the Hapi flooding the valley (Kuiper, 2011).

g. Kemetic scholars were indeed aware of history, which they used to evaluate the per-Aas, among its other uses.

- The recording of the King's list is one such example.

h. It was during the Early Period in Kmt that the Kemites had kings who ushered in the concept writing into Kmt and the first known government administrations.

i. The Kemetic style of art along with writing was developed during the Early Period (ca. 3100 – 2160 B.C.E.).

j. Papyrus as a writing material appeared some time during the First Dynasty (ca. 3100 B.C.E.) (Kuiper, 2011). Author, naturalist, and philosopher Pliny the Elder described how paper was made from papyrus. Pliny's description would seem to suggest he may have witnessed paper being made from papyrus.

k. Regarding legal proceedings in Kmt (Kuiper, 2011):

- The Kemites had no legal representation because they represented themselves.

- People had to present evidence proving their case(s), and could also call witnesses, rather than hiring attorneys, court appointed or otherwise.

DR. IAN SHAW

BRIEF AUTHOR BIO

- Prof. – Dept. Archaeology, Classics, and Egyptology – University of Liverpool

- Fmr. Chair of the Egypt Exploration Society

- Completed Ph.D. dissertation on the Amarna period of Ancient Egypt

- Authored other titles on ancient Egypt, such as *Egyptian Warfare and Weapons*

Sources:
liverpool.ac.uk/archaeology-classics-and-egyptology/staff/ian-shaw/
en.wikipedia.org/wiki/Ian_Shaw_(Egyptologist)

THE OXFORD HISTORY
OF ANCIENT EGYPT

MANUSCRIPT TYPE: Book

Main Points from the Text:

a. The earliest known use of writing in Kmt quite possibly preceded Upper and Lower Kmt being unified as one nation.

- Seshu (scribes), as well as artisans, were already writing in Kmt by Dynasty 0 (ca. 3200 – 3000 B.C.E.) (Shaw, 2003).

- Shaw (2003) also stated his disagreement with scholars who have attributed the origins, so to speak, of Kmt's writing system more or less exclusively to Mesopotamia.

  He wrote:

"...the two writing systems are so different that it seems more likely that they are both the result of independent invention" (p. 74).

b. The discovery of what are referred to as the Hekanakhte/Heqanakht Papers come to us from the Middle Kingdom period in Kmt.

- What makes these papers a focal point here is that the letters included correspondence in the form of a letter from a woman to her mother (Shaw, 2003).

- It was argued that this woman could have easily had a male scribe write the letter for her, and that most men would have taken this course of action.

c. There were mentions made by other sources regarding female seshu during the Middle Kingdom period:

"References to two Middle Kingdom female scribes suggest that a few women may nevertheless have been literate at this date" (Shaw, 2003, p. 151).

- Author and theologian Dr. M. Christine Tetley also talked about the Hekanakhte/Heqanakht Papers, and mentions a Kemetic female scribe. Tetley (2017) commented:

    "The letters were written by Hekanakhte and an associate, a lady called Sitnebsekhtu (otherwise spelled Zat-Neb-sekhtu), apparently in Memphis..." (p. 347).

d. It was during the Middle Kingdom that there was an expansion of bureaucracy under Senusret III (ca. 1881 B.C.E.), which in effect saw the appearance of various literary forms.

    - This same period was considered the *classical era* of Kemetic literature (Shaw, 2003).

e. During the Middle Kingdom period, literacy was more common place than during the Old Kingdom period.

f. Writing from Dynasty 0 had both economic and administrative importance to the early royal governing of Kmt.

DR. JOHN BAINES

BRIEF AUTHOR BIO

- Prof. Emer. of Egyptology – Oxford University

- Member – American Philosophical Society

- Received his Ph.D. from Oxford University

- Other publications include *Cultural Atlas of Ancient Egypt* & *Principles of Egyptian Art*

LITERACY

&

ANCIENT EGYPTIAN SOCIETY

MANUSCRIPT TYPE: Research Article

Main Points from the Text:

a. Very few people in ancient Kmt were literate schooling was limited.

   ▪ In order to have a truly administrative government, there had to be very few literate people (Baines, 1983).

b. The creation of mdu nTr began toward the end of the Pre-Dynastic period (ca. 5000 – 2950 B.C.E.) but reached its completed form during the First Dynasty (ca. 2950 B.C.E.).

c. The idea to develop a writing system arrived in Kmt in a roundabout way or *stimulus diffusion* from Mesopotamia (Baines, 1983).

d. The fact that mdu nTr developed as quickly as it did is quite compelling.

e. The field of accounting had a dominant influence on the development of a written language in Kmt.

f. The centralization that occurred during the Old Kingdom stunted the growth of genres of writing in Kmt.

  - It was during the First Intermediate period in Kmt (ca. 2181 – 2050 B.C.E.) that one could see an increase in the number of biographical texts not authorized by the royal family.

g. During the Middle Kingdom period (ca. 2040 – 1784 B.C.E.), also referred to as the Literary age, one continued to see other genres of texts produced.

- Among these genres were wisdom texts and narrative stories.

h. The changes in writing in Kmt followed behind moments of upheaval, or what Baines referred to as transitions.

  - This was due to the fact that writing was part of the system of acceptable behaviors in Kmt.

  - In order for writing to have changed in Kmt, the system in which writing was being used also had to change.

i. Some of the elite in Kmt were not literate in the sense that they could not read mdu nTr.

j. By the First Intermediate period (ca. 2181 – 2050 B.C.E.), schools were in existence that taught basic literacy.

  - Concerning whether or not schools that taught basic literacy during the Old Kingdom or Pyramid

Age (ca. 2665 – 2160 B.C.E.) existed, Baines (1983) says:

> "...their [schools] existence is uncertain for the Old Kingdom" (p. 580).

k. The average or normal literate Kemite would be able skilled in using one or two forms of the Kemetic writing systems (Baines, 1983).

- This was due to the fact that different forms of mdu nTr were used in different contexts.

l. The development of writing in Kmt appeared to be connected to the elite class, and in some way to changes that society went through. As such, writing in Kmt passed through five different phases:

- Phase I – Writing is developed and is restricted to "governmental" use and for demonstrating and illustrating to the public (e.g. display on temples).

- Phase II – Old Kingdom period. More and more people learn to read and write mdu nTr. Writing can regularly be seen in the areas of law and religion (Baines, 1983).

- Phase III – After the First Intermediate Period. Artistically expressive Kemetic literature can be more readily found.

- Phases IV – New Kingdom period. The various types of Kemetic literature continued to grow in number, and the total of texts being written also increases.

- Phase V – During and after the arrival of the Third Intermediate Period. Different forms of mdu nTr begin to appear, and literacy becomes more heavily regulated.

ANNETTE IMHAUSEN

BRIEF AUTHOR BIO

- Received her Ph.D. in History of Mathematics – Gutenberg University - Mainz

- Also the author of *Mathematics in Ancient Egypt: A Contextual History*

- Prof. of Normative Orders Cluster of Excellence – Goethe University Frankfurt

- Was featured in the BBC TV production, The Story of Maths

Sources:
normativeorders.net/en/organisation/staff-a-z/person/131
en.wikipedia.org/wiki/Annette_Imhausen

ANCIENT EGYPTIAN MATHEMATICS: NEW PERSPECTIVES ON OLD SOURCES

MANUSCRIPT TYPE: Research Article

Main Points from the Text:

a. Writings that were produced regarding daily life in Kmt were thrown away after using them.

b. When Kemetic mathematical papyri were translated into modern mathematical concepts, their most powerful features were lost (Imhausen, 2006).

   ▪ It was not at all surprising to see the mathematical achievements of the Kemites viewed and referred to as crude, simple, or even primitive.

c. After writing his dissertation on Kemetic ways of calculating with fractions, Otto Neugebauer began studying Mesopotamian mathematics instead. Neugebauer was convinced that Mesopotamian mathematics was of "a higher level of scientific achievement" (Imhausen, 2006, p. 20).

- Neugebauer was of the belief that even though the Kemites had a highly developed civilization that grew and expanded for several hundred years, the Kemites did nothing to further develop the sciences.

Kmt just so happened to be affected by the mathematical genius that flowed from Mesopotamia as Neugebauer observed:

> "It is at this single center (Mesopotamia) that abstract mathematical thought first appeared, affecting, centuries later, neighbouring civilizations, and finally spreading like a contagious disease" (Neugebauer, 1975, p. 559).

d. Mathematical knowledge was not universal; being dependent on a cultural background in some way in order to develop.

e. There is evidence that came out of the Uj tomb in Aabdju (Abydos) of mathematics being used in ancient Kmt from prior to its being unified.

   ▪ The Uj tomb is thought to the burial site of Per-Aa Scorpion I (Imhausen, 2006).

f. In order to construct structures like the pyramids, mathematics was a necessary part for two reasons (Imhausen, 2006).

   ▪ Firstly, it was required develop the architectural plans.

   ▪ Secondly, it was needed to organize and divide the labor to build the pyramids.

g. The Kemites developed the term *mr* for pyramid and *sqd* to refer to sloped surfaces, such as those of the pyramids (Imhausen, 2006; Obenga, 2004).

h. There were several metrological systems (weights and measures) present in Kmt; many dating as far back as the Old Kingdom period (ca. 2665 – 2160 B.C.E.).

i. Kemetic scientists used very specific ways to calculate fractions (Imhausen, 2006).

   ▪ Instead of using a numerator and denominator, the Kemites used a special symbol to identify a fraction.

j. The Kemetic method of multiplication and dividing included the doubling of a particular number.

   ▪ The Rhind Papyrus and Lahun fragment UC 3159 contain specific examples.

k. Mathematical texts from the Middle Kingdom period (ca.2040 – 1784 B.C.E.) present a problem of some type, and then provide detailed steps on how to complete it.

l. Surviving mathematical texts that were written in Hieratic contain some 100 mathematical problems to solve (Imhausen, 2006).

- Imhausen provided a translation and example problem 56 in the Rhind Papyrus, which shows the style of Kemetic mathematics

m. Those who wrote the math problems often wrote the title in red ink, so the student could easily recognize the start of a problem.

n. The Kemites used vocabulary that distinguished between the types of mathematics (division, addition, multiplication, and so forth).

o. Learning mathematics was a practical matter, as it helped the Kemites with the division and handing out of rations, the volume of granaries, and so forth.

p. There are mathematical papyri that come from the New Kingdom (ca. 1554 – 1190 B.C.E.).

- The Wilbour Papyrus is one and contains the measurements and assessments of a field that covered a distance of 90 mi/145 km along the Hapi (Nile) (Imhausen, 2006).

E. A. WALLIS BUDGE

BRIEF AUTHOR BIO

- Was Curator of Egyptian & Assyrian antiquities – British Museum

- Was knighted in 1920

- Published a translation of the ancient Egyptian text, *Book of the Dead*

- Published his final work, *Fetish to God in Ancient Egypt* in 1934

Sources:
britannica.com/biography/Wallis-Budge
en.wikipedia.org/wiki/E._A._Wallis_Budge

A SHORT HISTORY OF THE EGYPTIAN PEOPLE

MANUSCRIPT TYPE: Book

Main Points from the Text:

a. Kemetic boys belonging to wealthy families were able to go to school (Budge, 1914).

   - Many of their fathers wanted their sons to become seshu (scribes) or even serve the per-Aa.

b. The local or village schools that existed taught the basic aspects of an education.

c. A student in Kmt often began school early in the morning and would finish around noon (Budge, 1914).

d. In the elementary schools, the students learned: reading, writing mdu nTr, copying passages on the subject of good morals, and showing respect for one's elders.

e. From the elementary schools, Kemetic boys then went to schools maintained by temples or the Government.

   ▪ In these schools, they were taught the necessary skills to begin working for the government upon completion of their studies (Budge, 1914).

f. Students who desired to be in the Civil Service often learned: "arithmetic, book-keeping, geometry, mensuration" (Budge, 1914, p. 208).

g. Students needed to have a solid understanding of not only the mdu nTr but also the Hieratic script too.

h. Copying the passages of sages from antiquity was meant to increase students' vocabulary and gradually better their handwriting.

i. Those who wanted to become employed in the temples also were required to study theology, mythology, medicine, astrology, and magic (Budge, 1914).

j. In the primary and secondary schools, students engaged in physical education of some kind, whether it was sports and/or playing games.

k. The position of scribe was not respected or idolized in some instances, for the learning it represented but instead for the power, wealth, and its high position in Kemetic society (Budge, 1914).

DR. JAMES E. HARRIS

&

DR. EDWARD WENTE

BRIEF AUTHOR BIO

- Dr. Harris is Prof. & Chmn – Medical School – University of Michigan Ann Arbor

- Dr. Wente is Prof. Emer. – Egyptology – University of Chicago

- Has x-rayed royal mummies, studying dental features

- Popular major publications include *Letters from Ancient Egypt*

Sources:
nytimes.com/1976/10/14/archives/the-grandmummy-of-king-tut-is-identified.html
en.wikipedia.org/wiki/Edward_F._Wente

AN X-RAY ATLAS
OF THE ROYAL MUMMIES

MANUSCRIPT TYPE: Book

Main Points from the Text:

a. Through the mummification process, the Kemites obtained a knowledge of anatomy, chemistry, and other arts and sciences (Harris & Wente, 1980).

b. By the end of the third dynastic period (ca. 2665 B.C.E.) or earlier, accidental exhumations (dig buried bodies from the ground) of previous burials convinced Kemetic priests and physicians that the burial practices then were not good enough and needed to be improved.

   ▪ Kemetic scientists began developing methods to preserve the body in a recognizable human form.

c. Mummification was practiced up until the early Coptic period.

- Later on in Kmt's history, mummification had become commonplace among Kemites from all social classes (Harris & Wente, 1980).

d. Classical writers, such as Herodotus and Diodorus, wrote about the mummification techniques that the Kemites developed.

- Herodotus had the following to say:

  "There are a set of men who practice that art [mummification] and make it their business. ... when a body is brought to them, [they] show the bearers wooden models of corpses...

  Herodotus continued:

  "...The most perfect way they say is to be after the manner of Him... the second way, which is inferior to the first and less costly; then they show the third [way] which is the cheapest..." (Harris & Wente, 1980, p. 5).

- Diodorus observed that:

  "... They have three manners of burial: one very costly, one medium and one modest... the Egyptians keeping the bodies of their ancestors in fine chambers, can behold at a glance those who died before they themselves were born..." (Harris & Wente, 1980, p. 6).

- Observations made by Herodotus and Diodorus regarding the Kemetic mummification process were more in line with practices during the New Kingdom (ca. 1554 – 1190 B.C.E.) and Late Kingdom (ca. 760 – 657 B.C.E.) in Kmt.

e. One of dehydrating agents that the Kemites used in the mummification process was natron, which is found naturally occurring in Kmt.

- Natron is composed of sodium carbonate and sodium bicarbonate(Harris & Wente, 1980).

- In mdu nTr, Natron was called *ntry*, which means 'the divine salt,' and was also used for purification and cleaning in Kmt.

- It is from the word *ntry* that the Greek term *nitron* is derived.

- Natron was also denoted by the Kemetic terms *hsmn*, *bd*, and *bsn*, which occurred in the Pyramid texts among other places.

f. Analyses of mummified bodies during the Middle Kingdom period (ca. 2040 B.C.E.) revealed the use of an oleoresin (mixture of essential oils and resin) used in the second mummification process described by Herodotus (Harris & Wente, 1980).

- The mummification process of the Middle Kingdom had improved upon that of the Old Kingdom.

- The use of Natron helped with the dehydration of the bodies.

g. A review of the New Kingdom mummified bodies agrees in almost every way with how Herodotus described the process that the Kemites had developed.

- Kemetic scientists were able to prevent decomposition of the bodies by dehydrating them with a solid type of Natron instead of the solution form.

- Hot resin was used and poured into the thoracic and abdominal cavities, so as to inhibit bacterial growth.

- The resin also acted as a disinfectant and deodorant.

h. The mummification process during the New Kingdom and Late Kingdom periods in Kmt consisted of thirteen steps (Harris & Wente, 1980, p. 19-25):

1) Putting the corpse on the operating table

2) Extraction of the brain

3) Extraction of the viscera (internal organs)

4) Sterilization of the body cavities and viscera

5) Embalming the viscera

6) Temporary stuffing of the body cavities

7) Dehydration of the body

8) Removing the temporary stuffing and washing body cavities

9) Packing body cavities with permanent dry stuffing materials

10) Anointing the body

11) Packing the face openings and body tissues

12) Smearing the skin with molten resin

13) Bandaging the body

i. Kmt was the source of the oldest medical text, which happened to be on anatomy.

- Kemetic priest from the Ptolemaic period (ca. 332 B.C.E.) Manetho stated that Hor-Aha (Athotis to the Greeks), the son of Per-Aa Mena/Menes, authored this text.

- The oldest text to exist is in the Turin Papyrus.

  - It is a magic creed or principle to protect against three different hazards common in Kmt: eye diseases, snake bites, and fish bones (Harris & Wente, 1980).

- Many of the medical texts may have been produced from much earlier medical treatises, possibly traced back as far as the Old Kingdom Period.

j. Kemetic scientists produced written texts with detailed information on the different subject they studied (Harris & Wente, 1980).

- The papyrus Smith deals with traumatology, gynecological remedies, and rejuvenation.

- The papyrus Kahun concentrates on gynecology and obstetrics.

  - It also includes sections on veterinary practices and mathematics.

- The papyrus Chester Beatty dealt with rectal diseases and spells against epilepsy.

- The Carlsberg Papyrus VIII focuses on ophthalmology (study of the eye), which so did the papyrus Ebers, and obstetric (relating to childbirth) prognostications (predictions/forecasts), similar to those in the Berlin and Kahun papyri.

- The Ebers papyrus focuses on multiple areas: exanthemata (rashes), diarrhea, melaena/melena (dark and sticky feces), intestinal worms, hematuria (blood in the urine), circulatory diseases, ulcers, and blisters

- Angina pectoris (chest pains) is also explained:

  "If thou examinest a man for illness in his cardia, and he has pains in his arms, in his breasts, and in one side of his cardia... it is death threatening him" (Harris & Wente, 1980, p. 56).

k. Kemetic physicians' observations were followed by a verdict or prognosis (Harris & Wente, 1980):

- I shall treat them

- I shall contend with it (ailment or disease)

- An ailment/disease not to be treated

l. Within the Edwin Smith papyrus, pathological anatomy is described in a manner that indicates a familiarity with anatomical parts of the body (Harris & Wente, 1980).

- Kemetic physicians stated that sprains are the result of the violent pulling of two members, each remaining in place.

- Therapies are also quite rational. Many dealt with: resting, removing splinters, sutures and/or adhesive taping, bandages and splints, and ways to reduce fractures and/or dislocations.

m. Cutters or *paraschist* in Greek, were not true physicians but they did possess anatomical knowledge (Harris & Wente, 1980).

- They were able to perform mummification procedures, such as removing the cranial content via the nostrils.

- It is no secret that their knowledge of the body was shared around.

n. Speaking of medicine, Kemetic doctors discussed the causes of diseases.

- Worms, pathogens, and psychic factors were among the causes talked about.

o. The medical profession has long been talked about as being a special calling in Kmt.

- The wooden panels of Hesyre (3rd dynastic period ca. 2665 B.C.E.) and the other forty-two known Kemetic physicians confirm this (Harris & Wente, 1980).

p. The majority of physicians in Kmt were linked to a state department, the palace, or the home of a noble.

q. Kemetic physicians often relied on apprenticeships passed down through families in order to obtain their education and study medicine.

r. Other afflictions that Kemetic physicians dealt with and wrote on included:

- Obesity

- Skin and hair issues

- Skeletal pathologies

- Soft tissue pathologies

PART III:

THE PEOPLE

OF

KMT

PHYSICAL CHARACTERISTICS

The human phenotype has been a matter of constant controversy and often heated discussion both in mainstream society and academic communities. By that, it is meant that the European and other non-Afrikan scholarly communities appear to have been focused, almost to the point of obsession, on proving that the Kemites and the ancient/classical writers wrong when they described the Kemites as a black skinned people.

Black skinned and woolly or kinky hair – were some of the words used by Herodotus to describe the Colchians; believing that they were descended from Kemites, specifically, from the soldiers of Per-Aa Senusret I (Sesostris to the Greeks).

Herodotus (2008) is quoted as saying that:

"It is in fact manifest that the Colchidians are Egyptian by race... several Egyptians told me ... the Colchidians were descended from soldiers of Sesostris. I had conjectured as much myself... firstly... they have black skins and kinky hair..." (p. 134).

Other classical Greek and Latin writers described the Kemites using phrases, such as *"thick lipped"* and *"kinky-haired."* Aristotle (1913) stated that people who were too black were cowards, and he then proceeded to name the Kemites (Egyptians) and Kushites (Ethiopians) as examples. He wrote:

"Too black a hue marks the coward, as witness Egyptians and Ethiopians... also too white a complexion... the hue that makes for courage must be... between these extremes. A tawny color indicates a bold spirit..." (p. 812[a]).

Speaking of the Ethiopians, classical writer and historian, Diodorus Siculus is cited by John Baldwin (1874) as coming to the following conclusion, *"the laws,* customs, religious observances, and letters of the ancient Egyptians closely resembled those of the Ethiopians, 'the colony still observing the customs of their ancestors'" (p. 276).

Rawlinson and Gilman (1920), inadvertently admitting that the Kemites were Black Afrikans while trying to dispute that very fact, stated:

"The fundamental character of the Egyptian in respect of physical type, language... is Nigritic. The Egyptians were not Negroes, but they bore a resemblance to the Negro which is indisputable... They were darker, had thicker lips..." (p. 24).

John Baldwin (1874), in his work *Prehistoric Nations*, had this to say about the ancient Kemites:

"According to the uniform testimony of tradition, civilization was first established in Egypt by colonies of Cushites, or Ethiopians. The old civilization throughout the whole upper valley of the Nile had the same origin..." (p. 272).

Dr. Cheikh Anta Diop (1991) pointed out that there were in fact two variants of the Black race: the straight-haired, who are represented by the Dravidians of Asia and the Nubians and the Tubbou or Tedda of Afrika, all of which have jet black skin, and the kinky-haired black Afrikans of the Equatorial regions of Afrika.

Both types of Black Afrikan variants were represented in the compositional make-up of the Kemetic population. Karl Richard Lepsius and Kurt Sethe reproduced a scene from the tomb of Ramses III, named the 'Table of Nations'. In another of his works, *Civilization or Barbarism*, Dr. Cheikh Anta Diop (1991) again mentions the 'Table of Nations' and said that it highlights how the Kemites saw themselves as black skinned. This document should have been the end of the discussion of whether Kmt was an indigenous Black Afrikan nation, as Diop and other Afrikan scholars have stated before.

The ancient Kemites did not and have never considered themselves separate in an ethnic sense from other Afrikans on the continent. The Kemetic artists would not hesitate to portray the genetic figure of the Kemite as Black. Dr. Diop even conducted melanin concentration tests of the skin of Kemetic mummies. From the melanin dosage tests, Dr. Diop revealed that the ancient Kemites were an undeniably Black Afrikan people.

The ancient Kushites (Ethiopians), undoubtedly a Black Afrikan people, remarked that the Kemites were descendants of theirs; saying that Kmt was a colony of Kush carried into Kmt by Asr (Osiris) (Diop, 1991; Houston, 2013). In her work, *Wonderful Ethiopians of the Ancient Cushite Empire*, Drusilla Dunjee Houston (2013) noted that the Kemites themselves said that their Ancestors came from the land of Punt (modern day Somalia), another Black Afrikan nation.

Nana Baffour Amankwatia II (Asa G. Hilliard III) (1995) wrote of the studies of Henri Frankfort, and his conclusions regarding the origins of the ancient Kemites.

Nana Baffour referred to Frankfort as one of those students of Kmt:

"...who recognized from the evidence that Egypt's cultural and historical antecedents were to be found 'south' of Egypt, deeper in the Nile Valley."

Frankfort also agreed:

"...that the population of the Nile Valley was homogenous physically and culturally, as much as a large group can ever be" (p. 85).

In his translation of Herodotus' work *The History of Herodotus Vol. I*, George Rawlinson highlighted precisely what the Greek historian of antiquity stated rather clearly: "... *it is certain that the natives of that country are black with the heat...*," speaking of the Kemites (p. 225). Dr. Diop (1974) cited Diodorus, in his work *African Origins of Civilization: Myth or Reality*, as saying the following: "*The Ethiopians say that the Egyptians are one of their colonies which was brought into Egypt by Osiris...*" (p.

1). Dr. Diop (1974) observed that those in antiquity who actually saw the Kemetic people confirmed the fact that they were Black Afrikans; writing that, as he indeed did, Herodotus insisting on various occasions that the Kemites were Black people.

Karl Baedeker (1914) also reminds us of Diodorus' statement on the Kemites and Kushites as well. Baedeker (1914) stated:

> "In classical antiquity the Egyptians were considered to be of African origin, and Diodorus has given expression to this view by quoting a tradition of the Ethiopians, according to which the Egyptians were originally an Ethiopian colony..." (p. xlix).

However, Baedeker (1914) takes it a step further by assuming, as so many other Eurocentric scholars have, that he knows better than the ancient writers and what they had seen or heard.

Dr. Diop (1974) cited Gaston Maspero, who summarized many of the ancient historians and their description of the Kemites in the following statement:

"By the almost unanimous testimony of ancient historians, they belonged to an African race [read: Negro] which first settled in Ethiopia, on the Middle Nile..." (p. 2).

For those who often try to discount Herodotus' description of the Kemites as a Black Afrikan people, how is it that they cannot admit that Herodotus was not blind or stricken with an inability to see, thus clearly being able to determine that the Kemites and even the Kushites were a Black Afrikan people with his own two eyes?

In his work, *The Story of Civilization: Our Oriental Heritage*, Will Durant (1963) claimed the following:

"No one knows whence these early Egyptians came. Learned guesses incline to the view that they were a cross between Nubian, Ethiopian and Libyan natives on the one side and Semitic or Armenoid immigrants on the other" (p. 146).

Durant asserted that no one knew where the early Kemites came from, but we know this to be false. For the Kemites themselves stated that they originated from the south; the interior of the Afrikan continent. So, it is interesting that Durant mentions black African groups in the make-up of the Kemetic population but then dodge the question, whether intentionally or not, of what the Kemites were in terms of their ethnicity.

Lewis Spence (1990), in his work, *Ancient Egyptian Myths & Legends* had this to say in his apparent confusion of who the Kemites were:

"That Egyptian [the language] is related to Semitic is practically certain, though here a racial problem intervenes and confuses, for the Egyptian race proper is not and never was, so far as can be ascertained, Semitic in type..." (p. 182).

It is clear that while Spence recognized that there was a relationship between the Kemetic language and Semitic type languages, he also knew that the ancient Kemites were not a Semitic people. Eugen Georg (1931), in his work *Adventures of Mankind*, stated quite clearly what the Kemites looked like and who they were: "... *Blacks were the first to plow the mud of the Nile, they were dark skinned, curly haired Kushites*" (p. 44)

Georg (1931) leaves very little doubt as to what the Kemites looked like, more importantly who they looked like; the Kushites to the south. E. A. Wallis Budge (1928) remarked the following about the term Ethiopian:

"... *classical historians and geographers called the whole region from India to Egypt, both countries inclusive, by the name of Ethiopia, and in consequence they regarded all the dark skinned and black people who inhabited it as Ethiopians*" (p. vii).

Aidan Dodson (2000) observed that "*Negroid features are to be found in the areas of the ancient kingdom that penetrated deep into the modern Sudan*" (p. 4). Dodson (2000) appears to have neglected to or perhaps thought it not relevant to the topic to offer any other details related to the phenotype of the Kemetic population other than skin tones.

Like so many other European writers, Dodson leans toward the conclusion and thus explanation that the indigenous Kemetic population was subject to repeated immigration, both peaceful and aggressive in what seems to be an attempt to say that the Kemites were not black Afrikan people. Walter Emery (1961) stated that the Kemetic people "... *during the period of the First Dynasty... were probably in the main racially separate, being descendants of the indigenous inhabitants of the Nile valley...*" (p. 110 -111).

Let us consider one more piece of information here brought forth by Dr. Cheikh Anta Diop. It is revealed that the Kemetic word denoting royalty in the etymological sense, means *(he) who comes from or is a native of the south.* Dr. Diop (1991) also reported that as the Muslim individual will turn toward Mecca; their holy place, so the Kemites turn toward the South; the land of their Ancestors. It is a known fact that those in the south were a Black Afrikan people. The Kemites themselves have repeatedly proclaimed where they hail from; where their Ancestors are from; that they were a proud Black Afrikan civilization.

Plate 1: Relief of Amun – Waset (Luxor) Museum

Plate 2: Statue of Per-Aa
Tutankhaten/Tutankhamen – Cairo Museum

Plate 3: Fishermen – Saqqara

Plate 4: Combat Practice - Saqqara

Plate 5: A Farmer - Saqqara

SOCIETAL LIFE

It becomes quite obvious from reading much of the literature surrounding Kemetic societal life that there is no consensus in the European community of scholars on a number of points related to Kemetic society; its origins, its functions, etc. However, there was one matter that many European scholars in particular appear to be in agreement on; *Kmt's origins were not from within Afrika.* As Dr. John G. Jackson (2001) once wrote:

> *"Several Egyptologists have theorized that the ancient Egyptians originally came from Asia... the only reason this thesis has been entertained is that it was fashionable to believe that no African people were capable of developing a great civilization..."* (p. 93).

Another example being that European and other non-Afrikan scholars still cannot agree on whether or not only boys, or both boys and girls were allowed access to an education. Additionally, these same scholars differ wildly in their descriptions of how daily life in Kmt carried on. Some have offered descriptions of oppressive and despotic per-Aas, while others have painted pictures of Kemetic society that are closer to what the evidence reveals.

African scholars have not found it necessary to engage in debate or serious discussion regarding the erroneous claim of a hereditary caste system in Kmt. There are scholars, such as Dr. Theophile Obenga and Dr. Runoko Rashidi, to name a few, who are convinced that there was no hereditary caste system in Kmt. Dr. Cheikh Anta Diop (1987), in similar fashion, thought that a caste system may have developed in Kmt; stating that the caste of India was based on and a corrupted version of that in Kmt. In his writings, there does not seem to be any mention by Dr. Diop of it being a hereditary caste existing in Kmt.

Herodotus (2008) also stated that there were castes, and gave the following list of seven 'castes' in his work

The Histories: Priests, Warriors, Cowherds, Swineherds, Retailers, Translators, and Pilots. While there was no caste system or social ranking of society based on heredity, there was a definite class hierarchy or social stratification that was abided by in Kmt. The social stratification in Kmt was as follows:

Royal Family

Priests, Warriors, and Government Officials

Artisans and Skilled Workers

Peasants and Farmers

Steele and Steele (1909) had also replied that Kmt was separated into distinct classes (King, Priests, Military, and Lower classes); with the priest class having tight control over education. Furthermore, Steele would have one believe that more often than not, Kemites could rise no higher than the class into which they were born. Other Europeans writers, such as John Kendrick (1852) have told us that those Kemites of a 'lower caste' in Kmt were never allowed to enter the 'higher castes' due to the 'caste' he or she was born too. In addition, Kemites from the 'lower castes' were excluded from the rising to a 'higher caste' for lack of specialized skills (Kendrick, 1852).

Emery (1961) described a total of three different social classes in Kmt that were present during the first two dynasties, and went further to say that the general conclusion on the social system, since there is a dearth of evidence available on it, is that it was on the whole feudal with the large serf population being comprised of indigenous Kemites serving a superior upper class of an undisclosed race. Emery (1961) appeared convinced that a social change of some sort brought the serf class in closer contact with the 'elites,' and this caused a mixing of the races and classes.

Budge (2016) expressed similar thinking, mentioning lower class and upper class in his remarks concerning Kemetic daily life. Elisee Reclus (1892), on the other hand, does not mention caste but instead relays to us that ancient Kmt fell into a period of decadence in which slavery was rampant, using the 'national records' as a source that confirmed Kmt's state of constantly enslaving others.

Reclus added that prior to this period of degradation and wide spread practice of enslavement, the Kemites must have went through an autonomous and independence stage of development, thus becoming civilized. Reclus points to the Great Pyramids as proof positive of his claim. It makes little sense that a nation at this time, so committed to the enslavement of its people and other forms of social degradation, could have spared the manpower and devoted the time necessary for the development of the arts and sciences.

In refutation of Reclus' argument, evidence can be found within the work *Ancient Egypt: From Prehistory to the Islamic Conquest*, edited by Kathleen Kuiper. Kuiper (2011) reported that slavery was in fact not at all common, being mostly restricted to captives and foreigners. She went even further to proclaim that those who were enslaved would marry into their owners' families, thus allowing enslaved person entry into free society. It is clear today that the literature and evidence available to us today refutes Reclus' and the 'national record's' conclusion.

It is not or it should not be any secret that while there were patriarchal elements present, the Ancient Kemetic social fabric and organization was matriarchal (Diop, 1974). Women in ancient Kmt enjoyed and commanded a great deal of respect. It was commonplace for women to buy, sell, and own property. According to Dr. John G. Jackson (2001), Herodotus wrote that Kemetic women would go to the market to trade and purchase goods; their husband would remain at the home.

It is also reported that women were able to file lawsuits and even participate as witnesses in legal proceedings; not needing any permission from their husbands to do so (Kuiper et al., 2011). Dr. Jackson (2001) also stated that Diodorus Siculus took note of the matriarchal behavior of the Kemetic royal family at the time, as well as that of the commoners. Diodorus is quoted as stating:

> "Among the private citizens, the husband by the terms of the marriage agreement, appertains to the wife, and it is stipulated between them that the man shall obey the woman in all things..." (Briffault, 1931, p. 279; Jackson, 2001, p. 94).

Durant (1963) wrote that men in Kmt married their sisters not because of any sort of romance born out of familiarity or incest, but due to their desires to access the family inheritance, which is passed down from a mother to the daughter. Kuiper (2011), on the other hand, is convinced that such marriages were confined to the royal families, and not those of the general population in Kmt. She added that most marriages among the general population in Kmt were monogamous with no official ceremony.

At one point in antiquity, according to Durant (1963), divorce was a right granted to both husbands and wives. Under the rule of the Ptolemies, that is believed to have changed, and due to the influence of the Ptolemies, divorce became an absolute right of the husband. It would seem, according to Durant (1963), that this change in tradition was only accepted by the 'upper class,' while the general population of Kmt was said to have kept with Kemetic matriarchal traditions. Kuiper (2011) added on the topic of divorce that it was easy to do but very expensive.

Interestingly, Budge (2016) pointed out that while polygamy was practiced mainly by the upper class in Kmt, the introduction of multiple wives into the household did not cause any domestic unrest, as the Kemites were known for being very affectionate in their marital relations. In *Monarchs of the Nile*, Aidan Dodson

(2000) reported that women in Kmt enjoyed a higher social status compared to that of other women in the ancient world at that time.

Dodson (2000) continued on to say that "*Although restricted in the range of occupations open to them, they appear to have been fully competent at law... without the need to be under the tutelage of a male*" (p. 5). In concluding on the matter, Dodson pointed to the fact that Kemetic women could hold the throne at all as a testament to the treatment and great respect afforded to women in Kmt.

Plate 6: Ipet-Isut (Karnak Temple) – Was the education headquarters during its time.

Plate 7: Ast (Isis) is in the seated position to give birth. Behind her are surgical instruments that were used by Kemetic physicians. – Kom Ombo Temple

Plate 8: A section of the Kemetic calendar – Kom Ombo Temple

Photo by Brian J. McMorrow.

Plate 9: Amenhotep Son of Hapu as a scribe –
Waset (Luxor) Museum

Plate 10: Ptahshepses as a scribe – Imhotep
Museum

Plate II: The Kemetic couple of Meryre, who was
a scribe and his wife Iniuy – Cairo Museum

Plate 12: A Kemetic woman thought to be the wife of Nakhtmin who was a royal scribe – Cairo Museum

GLOSSARY

OF

TERMS

GENERAL TERMS

Abacus: - A mathematical instrument used to perform basic calculations made up of a square frame, rods, and beads that slide along the rods.

Admonition: - Advice, caution, or a warning given to someone about something that they have done or should do.

Aerofoil/Airfoil: - A curved surface created to help lift or control aircraft by utilizing the surrounding air currents.

Animal husbandry: - An agriculture science that deals with the farming of domestic animals in order to produce meat, milk, etc.

Arithmetic: - The basic subsection of mathematics that deals with the process or ways of completing simple calculations, such as multiplication, addition, division, or subtraction.

B.C.E.: - Before (the) Common Era.

Bureaucracy: - A system of governing or controlling an organization, company, or country by large numbers of bureaus, government administrators and officials.

Ca/Circa: - Around; about; approximately. Used when discussing dates.

C.E.: - (The) Common Era.

Clepsydra: - An ancient device that was used for measuring the flow of liquids into or out of a vessel.

Constellation: - Western astronomy defines a constellation is collection of stars that are arranged in a pattern that have been given a name. In astrology, a constellation is a group of stars that form at a specific moment (seasons, birthdays, etc.) that may affect events, behaviors, etc.

Coptic writing: - Said to be the final phase of development of the ancient Kemetic (Egyptian) language that was written using the Greek alphabet and some characters from the Kemetic demotic writing system.

Cosmogony: - The study of the genesis and evolution of the universe or a specific part of the universe.

Demotic writing: - The cursive form of the mdu nTr (medu neter) writing system that replaced hieratic writing. Demotic writing was used for business purposes, writing literature, and other daily writing activities.

Dewey Decimal System: - A system for organizing library content by separating books into 10 main subject groups.

Dietetics: - A branch of science that deals with the study of people's nutritional planning and preparation of meals and its influence on health.

Ecclesiastic: - A person who belongs to a religious group's leadership; often used to refer to Christian priests or other Christian church officials.

Epagomenal: - Used to describe days that were inserted into the Kemetic solar calendar at regular time periods.

Epicenter: - The focal point of an activity or situation.

Epoch: - A lengthy period of time that is typically marked by a series of major historical events.

Etymological: - Having to do with the study of words; a history of their beginnings and development.

Equilibrium of the lever: - A lever is said to reach equilibrium when the force that is applied to each arm with regard to its center are equal.

Exanthema: - A skin rash that occurs as a symptom of a disease, for example, the measles or chicken pox.

Exhumation: - The process of removing a deceased body from the ground after its burial; usually performed to discover how a person died.

Fellahin: - Coming from the Arabic word fallah meaning peasant.

Four cardinal points: - The four major directional points of a compass; north, south, east, and west.

Geodesist: - A person that deals with figuring out the size, shape, precise geographical points, and curvature of Earth.

Gynecology: - The field of medicine that deals with the health, physical care, and diseases of women; particularly that of a woman's reproductive organs.

Hekanakhte/Heqanakht Papers: - Letters from the Twelfth Dynasty (ca. 1961 – 1917 B.C.E.) said to have been written by Hekanakhte/Heqanakht of Waset (Thebes) and a woman associate named Sitnebsekhtu. Said to be included in the Hekanakhte/Heqanakht papers was a letter from a woman to her mother, indicating that women in Kemet were literate as well as men.

Hematuria: - The existence of blood in urine.

Hieratic writing: - The cursive form of the mdu nTr writing system that was used from the First Dynasty (ca. 3100 B.C.E.) until approximately 200 B.C.E. It is thought to have been a better fit for writing on papyri.

House of Life: - See per ankh under Kemetic terms.

Hyksos: - Also referred to as the *"Shepherd Kings,"* the Hyksos are thought by some scholars to be nomadic invaders from Asia who attacked and occupied Kemet during the fifteenth, sixteenth, and seventeenth dynasties (ca.1730 – 1560 B.C.E.), and were finally expelled from Kemet in the eighteenth dynasty.

Ideogram: - A written character that symbolizes something, such as an idea or thing.

Imperishable stars: - Referred to as *"Ikhemu-sek"* in the ancient Kemetic language, imperishable stars are assumed to be Northern circumpolar stars that never drop below the horizon.

Indefatigable stars: - Also called "*Ikhemw-wredj*" in the ancient Kemetic language, indefatigable stars are those that were rising and setting in the southern skies.

International Nubian Rescue Mission: - An organization that reclaimed and restored ancient artifacts and monuments prior to the Nubia region being flooded by the Aswan Dam.

Inundation: - To cover or overwhelm an area with water; flood.

Insatiable: - The state of wanting more; unable to be satisfied or pleased.

Jurisprudence: - The study of the philosophy and science of law.

Kiln: - A type of oven that is typically used to bake or dry objects made of clay, such as pottery.

Levant: - A term used to refer to the geographical regions of the Eastern Mediterranean section of Western Asia made up of current day Lebanon, Israel, and Syria.

Liturgy: - A group of rituals consisting of actions, words, or music utilized for public worship.

Maroons: - Groups of Africans who were enslaved in the Americas, who refused to remain enslaved and escaped and formed their own free communities.

Maxim: - A statement that is considered an essential moral principle, rule or general truth about how one should behave.

Melaena/Melena: - The passing of dark and thick stools with the presence of decaying blood that often indicates bleeding in the upper area of the digestive tract.

Meninges: - The three different very thin tissue layers that cover the both the brain and spinal cord.

Mensuration: - The subsection of geometry that deals with the process of measuring length, volume, or area.

Metempsychosis: - The migration of one's soul at death to a new body or vessel, thus beginning the soul's new phase of existence.

Narmer palette: - Sometimes referred to as the Palette of Narmer, the Narmer palette is a plate containing decorated inscriptions showing the First Dynasty Per-Aa Narmer battling and defeating his foes.

Nilometer: - A pillar that is used as a gauge to measure the rising and falling of the Hapi (Nile) river in Kemet.

Nome: - One of the 42 main administrative provinces of ancient Kemet.

Observatory: - A place where astronomers are able to observe and analyze planets, stars, and other natural developments. Modern day observatories often have a very large telescope that the astronomers use to make their observations.

Obstetrics: - A subsection of medicine that focuses on pregnancy and childbirth, and the treatment of and care for women during and after childbirth.

Oleoresin: - A partially solid mixture of natural essential oils and resin created from specific plants.

Ophthalmology: - A subsection of medicine that focuses on the structure, functions, and illnesses associated with the human eye.

Orthogonal projection: -

Osirica: - A "grand lodge," which was located in Lower (Northern) Kmt, which was devoted to the worship of the manifestation of the Creator, Asr.

Palermo Stone: - Re-discovered in the Italian city of Palermo, it is considered one of the fundamental sources used in the study of ancient Kemetic history.

Papyrus: - A tall plant that is widely grown near water in the Eastern Delta area of Kemet from which a paper writing material was made.

Pedagogical: - Having to do with the approaches, standards, and theories used to teach or with education in general.

Phenotype: - The outer physical traits of a living creature dictated by its genes' interaction with its environment that are visible to the eyes.

Phonogram: - A written character that symbolizes sounds.

Physiologoi: - Individuals that observed and asked about the nature of something; nature philosophers.

Polytheism: - The belief in or worship of a variety of different gods or goddesses.

Prognathous: - Possessing a jaw that extends beyond the upper region of one's face.

Priapism: - A condition of the penis characterized by a sustained and very painful erection. Priapism is sometimes caused by blockages in the blood vessels of the penis as well as neurological diseases.

Prognosticate: - To foretell or pass judgment on future events based on current clues or evidence.

Pugilist: - Someone that fights, most often professionally, using their fists; a boxer.

Ramesseum: - A funerary or memorial temple dedicated to Per-Aa Ramses II (the Great), constructed on the western bank of the Hapi (Nile) river. The ancient Kemites referred to this temple *"The Temple of Millions of Years Usermaatre that Unites with Waset."*

Rhetoric: - The art of using speech or writing in an effective manner with the intention of influencing and convincing others of something.

Sarcophagus: - A coffin made of stone that was often decorated and at times had inscriptions on them.

Scorpion mace-head: - A blunt club type weapon thought to belong to Per-Aa Scorpion from Dynasty Zero (ca. 3300 or 3200 B.C.E. possibly) that was re-discovered in 1898.

Sothic cycle: - According to the Kemetic solar calendar, a Sothic cycle was a complete period of 1,460 years each containing 365 days.

Stimulus diffusion: - The process by which various aspects of one culture spread to another culture and become transformed in some way.

Stone ostraca: - Broken pieces, usually of pottery, containing an inscription of some sort.

Sumerian: - Thought to have been developed and utilized during the third millennia B.C.E., it was the first written script used in the southern region of ancient Iraq.

Traumatology: - A subsection of surgery that involves the analysis, investigation, and treatment of serious and severe wounds or injuries usually caused by some type of violence or accident

Treaty of Westphalia: - A series of treaties that saw an end to the wars being fought in Europe over religion, namely what are referred to as the *Eighty Years' War* and the *Thirty Years' War*.

Truncated pyramid: - A pyramid that has had its apex or point cut off and removed.

KEMETIC TERMS

**Some of the Kemetic terms below have phonetic spellings in parenthesis for pronunciation assistance.

Ab: - Symbolizes the human heart and was believed to be the seat of the soul.

Akhet/Akhit: - The season of flooding or inundation in Kmt.

Ankh: - Represents life, whereas ankh the object represented the key of life.

Ater: - See *Itr.*

Ba: - Represents consciousness and refers to the human soul.

Djed (jed): - Represents the Kemetic concept of stability.

Djnnt (jen-net): - A medical term that means skull or cranium.

Gma (geh-mah): - Meaning temporal bone(s). The temporal bones are situated on either side of the human skull.

Heheh: - Represents the Kemetic concept of eternity.

Heru: - Usually translated as "he who is above" or "the one on high," Heru was known to the Greeks as Horus. Heru is a manifestation of the Creator that was often shown with the head of a falcon in Kemetic history, and was the son of Asr (Osiris) and Ast (Isis).

Hotep: - Meaning offerings, satisfaction, peace, and greetings. Can also be written as hetep.

Ikhmw-sek (ee-khe-moo-sek): - See Imperishable stars.

Ikhmw-wredj (ee-khe-moo-wrej): - See Indefatigable stars.

Imy-r-swnw (ee-mee-er soo-noo): - A doctor who was a manager or supervisor in Kmt.

Inm (ee-nem) - A word used in reference to the color or shade of a person's skin.

Itr (ee-ter): - A unit of measurement used in Kmt that was the equivalent of 20,000 cubits or 10.5 km

Ka: - The Ka represents the immortal essence or life force that reunites with the divinity after one's death

Kat: - The vagina (Obenga, 2015, p. 391).

Khepera: - Also said and written as Khepri, Kheper, Khephir, and Chepri, Khepera represents various ideas in Kmt, such as the creation of the Universe, transformation, rebirth, and ressurection.

Kmt (Keh-met): - One of the many names used by the Kemites to refer to their homeland misnomered Egypt.

Maat (ma-aht):- Represents balance, harmony, and doing what is right. The principles associated with maat were: right, truth, justice, good, balance, reciprocity, and compassion.

Mdu nfr (meh-doo neh-fer): - Good or beautiful speech.

Mdu nTr (meh-doo neh-ter/neh-cher): - Divine speech or words.

Meri: - Can mean beloved or love.

Mh-nsut (meh-nee-soot): - Also called the royal cubit, the mh-ni-sut was a unit of measurement use for smaller lengths, often equaling 52.3cm or approximately 20.6 inches.

Mh-Snt (meh-shent): - The mh-Snt was a unit of measurement used for measuring fields, equaling 100 cubits or approximately 45.7 meters.

Mndj (meh-nej): - The Kemetic term that refers to a person's breast.

Mr (mer): - A pyramid.

Mt (met): - Met had a multitude of meanings depending on the context, such as nerves, ligaments, tendons, and so on.

Neter/Netcher: - Refers to everything in existence. Neter can also have an interpretation similar to that of nature in English.

Ntnt (neh-teh-net): - The Kemetic term for the meninges that covers the human brain and spinal cord.

Per-Aa (per-ah): - A term used to refer to a king in Kmt. Per Aa can also be used to refer to a large house or building.

Per Ankh: - Meaning house of life in the Kemetic language. Per ankh was also used to refer to libraries, various types of schools/universities, clinics, temples, or seminaries.

Pr-m-Hru (per-em-heh-roo): - The title for *The Book of Coming Forth By Day and By Night*, misnomered *Book of the Dead*.

Peret/Perit: - The season of cultivating crops according to the Kemetic calendar. Also referred to as the season of emergence.

Sba (seh-bah): - Teaching or study. sbA can also refer to a teacher.

Seboyet: - A word that could mean instructions of learning or wisdom.

Seneb: - A word meaning wellness or health.

Sepat: - An administrative region in Kmt. Also called a nome.

Seshu (se-shoo): - A scribe or scholar.

Shd-swnw (shed-soo-noo): - A medical consultant.

Shemu (sheh-moo): - The season of the inundation or flooding of the Hapi (Nile) river in Kmt.

Shrt (she-ret): Refers to a nostril.

Sia (see-ah): - A term that can refer to insight, intuition or awareness.

Smsw-swnw (shem-soo soo-noo): - A term describing what would today be a registrar or senior physician in a hospital that manages the residents and interns.

Sqd (se-qued): - A term that means sloped or slanted surfaces, for example, the sloped sides of a pyramid.

Swnw (soo-noo): - A term that can mean doctor or a junior level doctor.

Ta-Seti: - A civilization located to the south of Kmt. Ta-Seti meant *land of the bow* and is considered by some to be the oldest civilization, even older than that of Kmt.

Udja (oo-jah): - A term that means prosperity.

Wab (oo-ab) – The socket of a tooth (Obenga, 2015).

Whmy Msw (weh-mee meh-soo): - A term that meant reawakening in the Kemetic language.

Wpt (oo-pet): - Refers to the top of a person's skull.

Wr-swnw (ur-soo-noo): - A term that is used to denote a senior doctor.

Wxdw (oo-khe-doo): - A term used to refer to the sensation of pain.

Zed: - Referring to that which decomposes after death.

BIBLIOGRAPHY

BIBLIOGRAPHY

SELECTED BOOKS & ARTICLES

1. Akbar, N. (1999). *Know thyself*. Tallahassee, FL: Mind Productions & Associates.

2. Akbar, N. (1994). *Light from ancient Africa*. Tallahassee, FL: Mind Productions & Associates.

3. Amen, M. M. (1975). Egypt, Libraries in. In A. Kent & H. Lancour (Eds), *Encyclopedia of Library and Information Science* (Vol. 7, pp. 574-588). New York, NY: Marcel Dekker Inc.

4. Amen, R. (2012). *A life centered life living MAAT*. Los Angeles, CA: Self Published

5. Aristotle. (1933). Metaphysics Vol. 1. (H. Tredennick, Trans.) New York, NY: G. P. Putnam's Sons.

6. Aristotle (1913). *The works of Aristotle*. (T. Loveday & E. S. Forster, Trans.) W. D. Ross (Ed.). Oxford, UK: Clarendon Press.

7. Asante, M. K. (2018). *The history of Africa: The quest for eternal harmony* (3rd ed.). New York, NY: Routledge.

8. Asante, M. K. (2000). *The Egyptian philosophers*. Chicago, IL: African American Images.

9. Baedeker, K. (1914). *Egypt and the Sudan: Handbook for Travellers* (7th ed.). New York, NY: Leipzig: Karl Baedeker, Publisher.

10. Baines, J. (1983). Literacy and Ancient Egyptian Society. *Man, 18(3)*, new series, 572-599. doi:10.2307/2801598

11. Baldwin, J. D. (1874). *Pre-Historic Nations*. New York, NY: Harper & Brother, Publishers.

12. ben-Jochannan, Y., & Simmonds, G. (2005). *The Black Man's North and East Africa*. Baltimore, MD: Black Classic Press.

13. ben-Jochannan, Y. A. A. (1989). *Black man of the Nile and his family*. Baltimore, MD: Black Classic Press

14. ben-Jochannan, Y. A. A. (1988). *Africa: Mother of Western civilization*. Baltimore, MD: Black Classic Press.

15. Bestetti, R. B., Restini, C. B. A., & Couto, L. B. (2014). Development of anatomophysiologic knowledge regarding the cardiovascular system: from Egyptians to Harvey. *Arquivos brasileiros de cardiologia*, *103*(6), 538-545. doi:10.5935/abc.20140148

16. Bresciani, E., Pernigottj S., Betrɋ M. C., Gallo, P., & Menchetti, A. (1983). *Ostraka demotici da Narmuti*. Pisa: Giardini.

17. Brier, B. M., & Hobbs, H. (2008). *Daily life of the ancient Egyptians*. Westport, CT: Greenwood Press.

18. Briffault, R. (1931). *The mothers: The matriarchal theory of social origins*. New York, NY: The MacMillan Company.

19. Brunner, H. (1991). *Altägyptische Erziehung*. Wiesbaden: Otto Harrassowitz.

20. Budge, E. W. (2016). *The dwellers on the Nile: Chapters on the life, literature, history and customs of the ancient Egyptians*. Mineola, NY: Dover Publications, Inc.

21. Budge, E. A. W. (1928). *A history of Ethiopia. 2 Volumes*. London, UK: Methuen & Co.

22. Budge, E. A. W. (1914).*A short history of the Egyptian people: With chapters on their religion, daily life, etc.* New York, NY: JM Dent & Sons

23. Clagett, M. (1995). *Ancient Egyptian science. Vol. II: Calendars, clocks, and astronomy.* Philadelphia, PA: American Philosophical Society

24. Clagett, M. (1999). *Ancient Egyptian science. Vol. III: Ancient Egyptian mathematics.* Philadelphia, PA: American Philosophical Society

25. David, R. (2003). *Handbook to life in ancient Egypt.* New York, NY: Facts On File, Inc.

26. Delany, M. R. (1991). *The origin of races and color.* Baltimore, MD: Black Classic Press.

27. Diop, C. A. (1991). *Civilization or Barbarism.* (Y. M. Ngemi, Trans.) H. J. Salemson & M. de Jager (Ed.). Chicago, IL: Lawrence Hill Books.

28. Diop, C. A. (1987). *Precolonial Black Africa.* (H. J. Salemson, Trans.). Chicago, IL: Lawrence Hill Books.

29. Diop, C. A. (1974). *African Origin of Civilization: Myth or Reality*. (M. Cook, Trans.). Chicago, IL: Lawrence Hill Books.

30. Dunlap, L. W. (1991). Libraries (History: Sumeria, Egypt and Assyria). In B. Johnson (Ed.), *Collier's Encyclopedia* (Vol. 14, 558-559). New York, NY: Macmillan Educational Company.

31. Durant, W. (1963). *The Story of Civilization: Our Oriental Heritage*. Vol. I. New York, NY: Simon & Schuster.

32. Durant, W. (1966). *The Story of Civilization: The life of Greece*. Vol. II. New York, NY: Simon & Schuster.

33. Elson, N. R. (2015). *MerKaBa: The Great Pyramid is the Tree Of Life: Ka Ab Ba: Secrets revealed in the Great Pyramid Mer Akhutu Kemetic technology for remaking ourselves as beings of light* (3rd ed.). Mattapan, MA: The Academy of Kemetic Education & Wellness, Inc.

34. Emery, W. B. (1961). *Archaic Egypt*. Baltimore, MD: Penguin Books Inc...

35. Encyclopaedia Britannica. (2020). Rhind papyrus. Retrieved from https://www.britannica.com/topic/Rhind-papyrus

36. Erman, A. (1927). *The literature of the ancient Egyptians*. London, UK: Methuen & Co. Ltd.

37. Erman, A. (1894). *Life in Ancient Egypt*. New York, NY: The MacMillan Company.

38. Evans, J. A. S. (1968). Father of history or father of lies; the reputation of Herodotus. *The Classical Journal, 64*(1), 11-17. Retrieved from www.jstor.org/stable/3296527

39. Finch III, C. S. (2011). *Echoes of the Old Darkland: Themes from the African Eden*. Decatur, GA: Khenti Inc.

40. Finch III, C. (2007). *The star of deep beginnings: The genesis of African science and technology*. Decatur, GA: Khenti, Incorporated.

41. Fischer-Elfert, H. W. (1984). Education. In D. Redford (Ed.), *The Oxford encyclopedia of ancient Egypt* (Vol. 1., pp. 438-442). New York, NY: Oxford University Press.

42. Flinders-Petrie, W. M. (1923). *Social life in ancient Egypt*. London, UK: Constable & Company LTD

43. Georg, E. (1931). *The adventure of mankind* (R. Bek-Gran, Trans.). New York, NY: E. P. Dutton & Co.

44. Gillings, R. J. (1982). *Mathematics in the time of the pharaohs.* Cambridge, MA: Academic Press Inc.

45. Gosse, A. B. (1915). *The Civilization of the Ancient Egyptians.* London:. T. C. & E. C. Jack.

46. Graves, F. P. (1909). *A history of education: Before the Middle Ages.* New York, NY: The MacMillan Company

47. Harris, J. E., & Wente, E. F. (1980). *An X-ray atlas of the royal mummies.* Chicago, IL: The University of Chicago Press

48. Heilbron, J. L. (2020). Geometry. Retrieved from https://www.britannica.com/science/geometry#ref726457

49. Herodotus (2008). *The histories.* (R. Waterfield, Trans.). New York, NY: Oxford University Press.

50. Herodotus (1909). *The history of Herodotus. Vol I.* (G. Rawlinson, Trans.). New York, NY: The Tandy-Thomas Company.

51. Hilliard III, A. G. (1998). *SBA: The reawakening of the African mind*. Gainsville, FL: Makare Publishing Co.

52. Hilliard III, A. G. (1995). *The Maroon within us*. Baltimore, MD: Black Classic Press.

53. Homer (2003). *The Odyssey* (Rev. ed.) (D. C. H. Rieu, Trans.). London, UK: Penguin Books Ltd.

54. Houston (2013). *Wonderful Ethiopians of the ancient Cushite empire*. New York, NY: New Timbuktu

55. Imhausen, A. (2006). Ancient Egyptian mathematics: New perspectives on old sources. *The Mathematical Intelligencer, 28*(1), 19-27.

56. Isocrates. (1928). *Isocrates in three volumes*. (G. Norlin, Trans.). Cambridge, MA: Harvard University Press.

57. Jackson, J. G. (2001). *Introduction to African civilizations*. New York, NY: Citadel Press

58. Jackson, J. G. (1990). *Ages of gold and silver and other short sketches of human history*. Austin, TX.: American Atheist Press.

59. Jackson, J. G. (1987). *The Golden Ages of Africa*. Clifton, NJ: African Tree Press.

60. James, G. G. M. (2001). *Stolen Legacy: Greek philosophy is stolen Egyptian philosophy* : Chicago, IL: African American Images

61. Kaplony-Heckel, U. (January 01, 1974). Schüler und Schulwesen in der agyptischen Spätzeit. *Studien Zur Altägyptischen Kultur*, 1, 227-246.

62. Kemp, E. L. (1902). *History of education*. Philadelphia, PA: JB Lippincott Company.

63. Kline, M. (1972). *Mathematical thought from ancient to modern times* (Vol. 1-3). New York, NY: Oxford University Press

64. Kline, M. (1963). *Mathematics: A cultural approach*. Reading, MASS: Addison Wesley Publishing Company.

65. Kuiper, K. (Ed.) (2011). *Ancient Egypt: From Prehistory to the Islamic Conquest*. New York, NY: Britannica Educational Publishing.

66. Laertius, D. (2018). *Lives of the eminent philosophers*. Cambridge, MA: Oxford University Press.

67. Lazaridis, N. (2010). Education and apprenticeship. *UCLA encyclopedia of Egyptology, 1*(1), 1-14. Retrieved from http://www.digital2.library.ucla.edu/

68. Lepsius, R. (1849). *Die Chronologie der Aegypter*. Berlin: Nicolaische Buchhandlung.

69. Levitt, J. I. (2015). The African origins of international law: Myth or reality. *UCLA Journal International Law and Foreign Affairs, 19*, 113, 1-35

70. Lichtheim, M. (2006). *Ancient Egyptian Literature Volume II: The New Kingdom* (2nd ed.). Berkely, CA: University of California Press

71. McCormick, P. J. (1915). *History of education: A survey of the development of educational theory and practice in ancient, medieval, and modern times* (2nd ed.). Washington, D.C.: The Catholic Education Press

72. McEvoy, T. J. (1915). *Epitome of history and principles of education* (2nd ed.). Brooklyn, NY: T. J. McEvoy

73. Metzger, P. A. (1980). The cover. *Journal of Library History*, 15(2), 210-212.

74. Montet, P. (1964). *Eternal Egypt*. London: The Trinity Press

75. Murison, R. G. (1951). *History of Egypt*. Edinburgh, SCT: T. & T. Clark

76. Nobles, W. W. (2008). Per Aa Asa Hilliard: The great house of Black light for educational excellence. *Review of Educational Research*, 78(3), 727-747. Retrieved from http://www.journals.sagepub.com/

77. Neugebauer, O. (1975). *A history of ancient mathematical astronomy*. M. J.Klein & G. J. Toomer (Eds.). Berlin: Springer-Verlag Berlin Heidelberg.

78. Obenga, T. (2015). *African philosophy*. Middletown, DE: Brawtley Press

79. Obenga, T. (2004). *African philosophy: The Pharaonic Period: 2780-330 BC*. Popenguine, SN: Per Ankh

80. Obenga, T. (1999). Africa, the cradle of writing. *The Imhotep Newsletter, 5,* 263-269. Retrieved from http://www.ankhonline.com

81. Obenga, T. (1996). *Icons of Maat.* Philadelphia, PA: The Source Editions.

82. Obenga, T. (1992). *Ancient Egypt & Black Africa.* (G. Pitcher & A. Sheik, Trans.) A. S. Saakana (Ed.). London: Karnak House.

83. Plato. (2005). *Euthyphro Apology Crito Phaedo Phaedrus.* (H. N. Fowler, Trans.). London, UK: Harvard University Press.

84. Plato (1892). *The Dialogues of Plato Vol. 5.* (B. Jowett, Trans.). London, UK: Oxford University Press.

85. Plato (1888). *The Timaeus of Plato.* (R. D. Archer-Hind, Trans.). London, UK: Macmillan.

86. Ptahhotep, Hilliard, A. G., Williams, L., & Damali, N. (1987). *The teachings of Ptahhotep: The oldest book in the world.* Baltimore, MD: Blackwood Press.

87. Rawlinson, G. & Gilman, A. (1920). *Ancient Egypt*. London, UK: T. Fisher Unwin LTD.

88. Reclus, E. (1892). *The earth and its inhabitants: Africa Vol. I*. A. H. Keane (Ed.). New York, NY: D. Appleton and Company.

89. Richardson, E. C. (1914). *Biblical libraries: A sketch of library history from 3400 BC to AD 150*. Princeton, NJ: Princeton University Press

90. Richardson, E. C. (1911). *Some old Egyptian librarians*. New York, NY: Charles Scribner's Sons

91. Roberts, J. (2017). Herodotus and the Greek identity. *Celebrating Scholarship & Creativity Day*. 110. Retrieved from https://digitalcommons.csbsju.edu/elce_cscday/110

92. Ruscio, J. (2006). *Critical thinking in psychology* (2nd ed.). Belmont, CA: Wadsworth.

93. Saber, A. (2010). Ancient Egyptian surgical heritage. *Journal of Investigative Surgery, 23*, 327-334. doi.org/10.3109/08941939.2010.515289

94. Sanchuniathon. (1720). *Sanchoniatho's Phoenician history: Translated from the first book of Eusebius de praeparatione evangelica: With a*

continuation of Sanchoniatho's history by Eratosthenes Cyrenaeus's canon, which Dicaearchus connects with the first olympiad. London, UK: Printed by W.B. for R. Wilkin.

95. Sarton, G. (1948). *The life of science: Essays in the history of civilization.* New York, NY: Henry Schuman

96. Schulz, R., & Seidel, M. (2004). *Egypt: The World of the Pharaohs.* R. Schulz & M. Seidel (Ed.). Konemann.

97. Shaw, I. (2003). *The Oxford history of ancient Egypt.* New York, NY: Oxford University Press

98. Siculus, D. (1989). *Diodorus Siculus, books 1-2.* (C. H. Oldfather, Trans.). Cambridge, MA: Harvard University Press.

99. Sifuna, D. N., & Otiende, J. E. (2006). *An Introductory History of Education.* Nairobi, KY: University of Nairobi Press

100. Smith, H. I. (1842). *History of education: Ancient and modern.* New York, NY: Harper & Brothers

101. Spence, L. (1990). *Ancient Egyptian myths and legends.* New York, NY: Dover Publications.

102. Steele, J. D., & Steele, E. B. (1909). *A brief history of ancient peoples*. New York, NY: American Book Company.

103. Stiefel, M., Shaner, A., & Schaefer, S. D. (2006). The Edwin Smith Papyrus: The birth of analytical thinking in medicine and otolaryngology. *The Laryngoscope, 116*(2), 182-188. doi: 10.1097/01.mlg.0000191461.08542.a3

104. Struik, D. J. (1948). *A concise history of mathematics*. New York, NY: Dover Publications.

105. Tetley, M. C. (2017). *The reconstructed chronology of the Egyptian kings*. Whangarei, New Zealand: B. W. Tetley.

106. The astronomical magnitude scale (n.d.). Retrieved from http://www.icq.eps.harvard.edu/MagScale.html

107. Thompson, J. W. (1982). *Ancient Libraries*. Berkeley, CA: University of California Press.

108. Tompkins, P., & Stecchini, L. C. (1971). *Secrets of the Great Pyramid*. New York, NY: Harper & Row

109. Van Loon, H. W. (1922). *Ancient man: The beginning of civilizations.* New York, NY: Boni and Liveright Inc.

110. Van Sertima et al. (1999). *Egypt revisited: Journal of African Civilizations.* I. Van Sertima (Ed.). New Brunswick, NJ: Transaction Publishers.

111. Van Sertima et al. (1999). *Great Black leaders: Ancient and modern: Journal of African Civilizations.* I. Van Sertima (Ed.). New Brunswick, NJ: Transaction Publishers.

112. Van Sertima et al. (1998). *Blacks in science: Ancient and modern: Journal of African Civilizations.* I. Van Sertima (Ed.). New Brunswick, NJ: Transaction Publishers.

113. Van Sertima, I. (1985). *Nile Valley Civilizations:. Journal of African Civilizations.* New Brunswick, NJ: Transaction Publishers.

114. Vernus, P. (1984). Schreibtafel. In W. Helck & W. Westendorf (Eds.), *Lexikon der Ägyptologie* (Vol. 5., pp. 703-709). Wiesbaden: Otto Harrassowitz.

115. Weisstein, E. W. (2018). Truncated Square Pyramid. Retrieved from mathworld.wolfram.com/TruncatedSquarePyramid.html

116. Wilkinson, J. G. (1878). *The manners and customs of the ancient Egyptians Vol. 1*. New York, NY: Dodd, Mead and Company

117. Williams, S. G. (1903). *The history of ancient education*. Syracuse, NY: C. W. Bardeen

118. Zaslavsky, C. (1999). *Africa counts: Numbers and patterns in African cultures (3rd ed.)*. Chicago, IL: Lawrence Hill Books

119. Zulu, I. M. (1993). The ancient Kemetic roots of library and information science. *Journal of Pan African Studies, 5*(1), 1-26. Retrieved from ERIC database. (ED382204)

Made in the USA
Coppell, TX
27 July 2023

19670353R00252